harvester of souls

JOHN NEUMANN

harvester of souls

JOHN NEUMANN

TOM LANGAN

OUR SUNDAY VISITOR, Inc.
NOLL PLAZA, HUNTINGTON, IN 46750

Cover Design by Eric Nesheim
Published, printed and bound in the U.S.A. by
Our Sunday Visitor, Inc.
Noll Plaza
Huntington, Indiana 46750

758

CONTENTS

TO MY WIFE
JULIE

ACKNOWLEDGMENTS

I wish to express my thanks to the late Reverend Michael J. Curley, C.SS.R., author of *Venerable John Neumann, C.SS.R.,* for his generous help in reading this manuscript and for offering valuable suggestions and corrections.

I also wish to thank the Reverend Francis J. Litz, C.SS.R., Vice-Postulator of the Cause of Blessed John Neumann, for making important source material available and for reading the manuscript and contributing his helpful comments and corrections.

I feel that these acknowledgments would not be complete without a word of thanks to my good friends, the late Victor E. Smith and his widow, Eva, who first introduced me to the story of John Neumann several years ago, when I visited them at their home at Maryfarm, Easton, Pa.

Tom Langan

CHAPTER ONE

On an April night in the year 1836, the three-masted ship *Europa* was plunging through heavy seas, en route from Le Havre to New York.

Standing at the rail was one of the passengers, peering into the black night. He was small of stature, standing only five feet, four inches in height. He was of stocky build and his clothes were shabby and worn. He had light brown hair, a large, broad forehead, and eyes that were penetrating and intense. His name was John Neumann, native of Prachatitz, a village in Bohemia. He was twenty-five years old.

Others among the 200 passengers on the *Europa* were sailing to North America to join relatives and friends, to seek a better life for themselves and their children and perhaps make a fortune. John Neumann was sailing to North America to be a missionary.

The United States was missionary territory at that time. Many priests journeyed from Europe to minister to the thousands of people who went overseas to America in giant waves of emigration. John Neumann had cherished the dream of being a missionary in America for three years. But now, when his dream was being fulfilled in the matter of making the voyage to America, it was keenly and painfully apparent to him that he was ill-equipped for his task. He was not yet an ordained priest.

He had completed his studies at the seminary in Prague the previous year, only to learn that no priests were being ordained from his class, and probably none would be ordained for a year. Apparently there was no shortage of priests in the area.

John Neumann tried to arrange for his acceptance as a missionary to America, but he met with frustration and disappointment. He attempted, through his contacts with European clergy, to get an assignment in Philadelphia, in New York, and in other areas, but with no definite result. He went to Paris, hoping meanwhile to receive news which would enable him to sail with a specific assignment. But he did not get confirmation on any of his prospects.

He had some money — the receipts of a collection taken up by priests in his native Prachatitz and vicinity — and a gift from the director of the seminary. But his funds were being depleted as he waited in Paris for definite word from America. And so he made his decision to sail, prayerfully and hopefully, into an unknown future.

Standing on the deck of the *Europa,* gazing into the blackness which shrouded the ship, he thought of his parents, and of his brother and four sisters. He recalled the sadness they felt, and the sadness he himself felt, when he told them of his plans to be a missionary in America. Despite the natural feeling of sadness, he knew they accepted his missionary work as something he felt called to do. But what would they think if they knew he was to arrive in America without any specific destination? Certainly that kind of planning, or lack of planning, would not meet with hearty approval from his father.

John's father, Philip Neumann, was a man of some importance in the village of Prachatitz. He was a stocking-maker. His business enabled him and his family to live in comfort, though not in luxury. He had served on the Town Council and also as Overseer of the Poor. He was a kind man, a just man, but a stern man when occasion required it. John vividly remembered a reprimand his father had once given him for lying.

Thinking of his mother, John remembered how she sometimes referred to him as her "little bibliomaniac," because of his fondness for reading. His mother was a devout woman who attended Mass daily and John often accompanied her. The atmosphere of the Neumann home was prayerful. In such a home, it was natural that John would think of the priesthood when it came time for him to decide on his life work.

His mother probably knew, with a mother's intuition, that he would study for the priesthood, long before he knew it himself. It was she who persuaded him to write a simple application to the seminary at Prague, when John was worrying about the fact that he might have difficulty in being accepted, since the applications were numerous and he had no influential friends to assist him. As things turned out, his application was all that he required.

John had remembered his mother in Paris. He had purchased some books, which he convinced himself he needed. They included a Greek Bible, a Spanish prayerbook, *The Works of St. Francis de Sales*, one book titled *Devotion to the Passion of Our Lord Jesus Christ*, and another called *The Spiritual Combat*. Then, in self-reproach, he wrote in his diary that he must curb this desire to have such possessions. And he recalled his mother's jocular description of him as her "little bibliomaniac."

Thinking on these things, John Neumann left the deck of the *Europa* and went below. It was time to write in his diary, a nightly habit begun in his seminary days. Unlike most diaries, which tell of lively parties and good times, John Neumann's diary was more like a record of his struggles, victories and defeats as he aspired toward perfection. It revealed a strong feeling of his own inadequacy, a great dependence on God and a keen desire to know and accomplish God's will. It also revealed an attitude of exactness and self-criticism which most people would regard as unduly severe. Overall, it was a careful record of the travail of soul John Neumann suffered while trying to find and follow the paths God wished him to travel.

The master of the *Europa,* Captain Drummond, had packed the ship with all the passengers it would hold. He even delayed the sailing date, so that he could have all the passengers and all the revenue possible. As a result of this crowding, there was not much privacy for anyone on board. Lying in his bunk, John Neumann wrote in his diary in Latin, to avoid the prying eyes of his fellow passengers. All his life he had been rather shy and retiring, and this manifestation of his shyness on shipboard did not serve to endear him to any of the other emigrants. They seemed to regard him as an odd character. He was studious, prayerful and thoughtful, and this, in the eyes of some of the coarser of the passengers, made him a fit subject for contempt.

"Yesterday and today," he wrote in his diary, "I made many good resolutions for my future. God gave me, also, an opportunity of practicing humility under contempt and insult. I bore it patiently, though with some violence to my feelings."

His diary had become like a mirror in which were reflected all of his inner conflicts and turmoil. During his student days he had written that he was annoyed with himself because by playing chess he had become distracted from the spiritual mood he wished to maintain. He was also annoyed because he had, in his strict opinion, an inordinate desire to win. He solved the problem in characteristic fashion by giving up chess.

When he was about to sail on the *Europa* he had become fearful of making the trip alone. Then, in self-reproach, he wrote: "But why this fear, as if there were no God!"

A storm buffeted the *Europa* for three days. Later, the ship was becalmed. At other times adverse winds prevented any forward progress.

John Neumann spent his time, through storm and calm, as diligently as shipboard life permitted. From his books he had chosen two for shipboard reading, the *Imitation of Christ,* by Thomas à Kempis, and *Philothea,* by St. Francis de Sales. He read them whenever and wherever he could find a bit of privacy and quiet. This habit of spending his time diligently was in line with a resolve he had made in his seminary days, never to waste a minute.

On land he liked to take long walks and he missed this exercise on the *Europa.* At the seminary he enjoyed long walks and long talks with his two friends, Adalbert Schmidt and Karl Krbecek. Now, he missed the walks and he missed the company of Adalbert and Karl. They had agreed to go with him to America as missionaries. But first Karl and later Adalbert made a different choice.

Although lonely for companionship, John Neumann seemed unable to make friendly contact with his fellow passengers. He did strike up an acquaintance with one German, and also with a Mexican boy with whom he could talk Spanish. This was one of the six languages, including English, with which John was familiar, in addition to his Latin and Greek.

In Spanish he had read the letters of one of the greatest of the missionaries, St. Francis Xavier. In one of his letters to St. Ignatius Loyola, written as he stood on the threshold of the Indies, St. Francis had written words which also fit John Neumann's attitude.

"One of the things which greatly comforts us and makes us hope increasingly for the mercy of God," St. Francis wrote, "is the complete conviction we have of lacking every talent necessary for the preaching of the Gospel in pagan lands. As anything we do is done for God our Lord alone, our hope and confidence grow greater daily that He will give us abundantly in His own good time whatever we need to promote His service and glory."

As the *Europa* continued on toward the port of New York and weary week followed weary week, John Neumann did his best to adjust to life on shipboard. Many a time he stood on the deck at night and studied the stars. Astronomy had been one of his favorite studies. He enjoyed it as one enjoys a hobby. He was a keen student of botany, too, and he liked to play the guitar. But these latter activities were no part of his life at sea. And so, he gazed silently at the heavens. The sight recalled to him a night when his younger brother, Wenceslaus, ran to his mother and complained that John would not go to sleep. His mother, thinking John might be ill, hurried into the bedroom and was greeted by John's troubled question: "Mother, how is it that our earth floats in the air without falling?"

"Let it float," his mother told him. "You do not have to hold it. God takes care of that. All you have to do is go to sleep and not disturb your brother."

Such thoughts of home came to John Neumann as he moved about the ship, going his quiet way, looking back at the past, recalling incidents of family life, incidents of his years as a student. A fellow student, in later years, recalled stubbornness as a character trait of John Neumann and this was probably accurate, if by stubbornness one means a resolute pursuit of predetermined goals. And this intent pursuit of goals, which today might be called a "drive," made of John Neu-

mann a very serious young man. He wasn't given to
clowning around or indulging in extrovert behavior. He
didn't dance. He rarely drank anything alcoholic. And
he once remarked to his friend Adalbert that women
were to him "beautifully bound books which I know not
how to read."

John Neumann had one feeling in common with his
fellow passengers. He found the trip wearisome and he
was anxious for it to come to an end. The *Europa* had
been sailing through fair weather and foul for almost
forty days. Provisions on the ship were low. There were
worms in the drinking water and it had a horrible odor.
Some passengers were ill. Some were quarrelsome.
Everybody on board felt the strain and uncertainty that
hovered like a storm cloud over the ship.

And then, on a May morning, a crew member shouted with gusto at the sight of a sea gull, foraging for
scraps of garbage in the wake of the ship. This was an
unfailing sign that land was not far away. The good news
spread and passengers lined the rails for hours, looking
off into the misty horizon.

"Land ho!" a lookout called and the passengers
yelled and danced with joy. Rain poured down on them
and they seemed not to be aware of it. Through the rain,
they could make out the shape of the shoreline, the
walls and roofs of houses, the spires of churches. The
Europa was off Staten Island, about an hour's sail to
New York.

Then came a shattering anticlimax. Captain Drummond decreed that they had to anchor right where they
were. Some of the passengers were ill, the Captain reminded them, and had to be cared for before disembark-
ing. Otherwise, the quarantine officials might decide
that the sick would have to be taken back to Le Havre.
In addition, the stormy weather made a landing at New
York hazardous. The Captain had spoken. They had to

remain anchored within sight of the land they had sailed forty days to reach.

The *Europa* lay at anchor off Staten Island for three days. Motivated by his "stubbornness," or perseverance, if you prefer, John Neumann asked the Captain six times during those three days if he could leave the ship. Six times the Captain refused permission. Finally, John Neumann was allowed to leave the *Europa* in a rowboat and he landed on Staten Island. He then sailed to New York on a small steamer.

It was the feast of Corpus Christi. John Neumann, wearing his shabby clothes and worn shoes, carrying his meager baggage and his treasured books, landed in New York at about noon. He had no hat. It had been stolen on shipboard. His funds were low. In terms of American money, he had about a dollar. It was raining.

But he was in America. His heart was filled with thankfulness to God for his safe voyage. And yet, in the back of his mind were the two nagging questions he had written in his diary the night before:

"What is in store for me?"

"What will my future be?"

CHAPTER TWO

John Neumann walked the streets of New York City in the rain, on that afternoon in June, 1836, and, like many an immigrant before and since, he marveled at what he saw.

New York City at that time had a population of 300,000. The life of the city was concentrated at the lower end of Manhattan Island, near the Battery. Broadway reached only to 25th Street, and this was considered far out of town. About six months before, a fire had raged through the city for two days, destroying the Stock Exchange, the Post Office and many other buildings. The fire caused property damage amounting to $20,000,000, but in spite of this scar on its economic life, New York City in 1836 was a bustling community.

John Neumann trudged through the rain, over cobblestone pavements and the mud of unpaved streets, carrying his baggage and his books. He was looking for a Catholic church. He wanted to kneel down in the presence of the Blessed Sacrament and thank God for his safe journey.

Several of the churches he saw were locked. He paused at one meetinghouse, which was open, but turned away when he saw a crowd of men coming out, smoking cigars and wearing their hats. He made several inquiries as to the location of a Catholic church, but no one he asked was able to help him. He saw a large barrel-shaped wagon pass along the street, and was amazed to learn that the barrel contained drinking water, which was for sale.

Night came on, and gaslight flickered on some of the street corners. Wet and weary, and somewhat bewildered by all the new sights and sounds, John Neumann decided to spend the night at an inn. He had not located a Catholic church, his future plans were shrouded in doubt as murky as the rainy night. But, he resolved, he would get up early in the morning and start anew.

The next day the innkeeper directed him to a Catholic church. It was a building recently bought from Protestants and was called Christ Church. Here, in the presence of his God, John Neumann poured out his feelings of gratitude. Then he sought out the pastor, Dr. Joseph Schneller, and got directions to St. Patrick's Cathedral. This was not the St. Patrick's Cathedral of today, on New York's Fifth Avenue. It was situated on Mott Street and was the heart of the episcopal see of Bishop John Dubois.

Bishop Dubois had come to America from France, a refugee from the terror of the Revolution in his native land. In his seventy-ninth year, he presided over the Diocese of New York, at that time a vast area which included all of New York State and part of New Jersey. The Catholic population in this huge territory was 200,000. Hundreds of immigrants, including many Irish and German, were arriving with each boat from Europe and this population increase, for the most part, was being registered in the Diocese of New York. Bishop Dubois was administering the diocese as best he could, with some thirty churches, augmented by services in fifty private homes. He had only thirty-six priests and could have used fifty more. Among the thirty-six priests, only three were German.

As John Neumann made his way to the cathedral,

the old doubts and fears which he had felt for weeks began to assail him again. He recalled that Canon Andreas Rass, director of a seminary in Strasbourg, had promised to write to Bishop Dubois about his serving in the New York Diocese, but John Neumann did not know for certain if Canon Rass had written Bishop Dubois, nor did he know what answer Bishop Dubois may have given the Canon, if any. The question at the root of John Neumann's doubts and fears was: If he were not accepted here in New York, if he were not ordained here, what then?

At the cathedral he met Father John Raffeiner, the vicar-general of the Germans in New York. John Neumann introduced himself and listened with mounting joy as Father Raffeiner welcomed him and told him that his offer to serve the Diocese of New York had been accepted three weeks before! Word of this had been sent to Canon Rass in answer to the Canon's letter. At the time, John Neumann was on the high seas. During those weary weeks aboard the *Europa* while he worried about his future, the matter had been resolved. His arrival in New York had been eagerly awaited!

Father Raffeiner took John Neumann to the two-story rented house which served as the episcopal residence. Bishop Dubois received him as though he were the answer to a prayer. He outlined plans to ordain the young aspirant as soon as possible. The bishop had to go out of town on a trip, an official visitation. He would ordain young Neumann in a matter of weeks, as soon as he returned. Meanwhile, the newcomer would work with Father Raffeiner, who was pastor of St. Nicholas Church on Second Street.

John Neumann left the presence of Bishop Dubois in high spirits. In his diary he registered his fervent feelings of thankfulness. Of his ordination he wrote: "I am seized with fear when I consider the sanctity of the office that awaits me and compare it with my own unworthiness."

He plunged eagerly into the work assigned him by Father Raffeiner, teaching catechism to a class of thirty children, as part of their preparation for First Communion. This was a task for which he was singularly fitted. He loved children and always got along well with them. Questions and answers fitted neatly into his orderly mind and he had a gift for communicating his knowledge to youngsters. John Neumann devoted himself zealously to instructing his charges.

On June 19 he was made subdeacon by Bishop Dubois, at St. Patrick's Cathedral. This was the first of the three major orders which he would receive in the process of becoming a priest. Writing in his diary, he promised to say the rosary every day of his life in honor of the Blessed Virgin, to secure her assistance in the discharge of his duties and to ask her protection over his family. He also wrote: "I shall map out my future in accordance with the rules of St. Francis de Sales." On June 24, the feast of St. John the Baptist, John Neumann was made a deacon and on June 25 Bishop Dubois ordained him a priest.

The next day, a Sunday, he said his first Mass, in St. Nicholas Church. The church was crowded, not only with those who wished to see the newly ordained priest say his first Mass, but with the thirty children who received their First Communion at the Mass, and with their families. Father Raffeiner preached the sermon and Father Neumann gave each of his little catechists First Communion. They were the first creatures of God with whom he made spiritual contact as a priest. This was the beginning of John Neumann's harvest of souls.

Father Neumann's ordination, an unforgettable experience for him, made no particular impact outside of his immediate circle. The Catholic paper published in

New York at the time gave the ordination two lines, misspelling his name, giving it as Newman. The young priest regretted that his parents and his brother and sisters could not have been present at his ordination and his first Mass. He wrote to them affectionately, penned lines in his diary telling of his spiritual exaltation, and then was ready for work.

Bishop Dubois could have used Father Neumann's services in several areas of his far-flung diocese. Near at hand, in Williamsburg and Harlem, there was an acute need for priests. On some nights, in crowded areas of the diocese, people would come to confession in such numbers that all could not be heard. In Utica and Rochester there was a need for German-speaking priests. And there were other communities where the lack of priests was a serious problem. Bishop Dubois had even started a seminary in Nyack, but the project was abandoned because of insufficient funds.

The bishop decided that Father Neumann would be most useful in the vicinity of Buffalo, near the northwest corner of the diocese. And there was no time for lengthy planning and preparation. Father Neumann was given new clothes by Father Raffeiner. Bishop Dubois gave him traveling expenses. And so, early on Tuesday morning, two days after he celebrated his first Mass, Father Neumann boarded a Hudson River steamboat and left for Albany, on the first leg of his journey to new duties, new complications. His attitude toward his work was reflected in an entry in his diary: "I must henceforth labor for the salvation of others."

The trip to Albany took twelve hours. The next day Father Neumann traveled to Schenectady by rail, and took passage on the canalboat *Indiana*. For four days the boat moved through the canal at a speed of four miles an hour, pulled along by horses walking on the riverbank.

As the *Indiana* arrived in Rochester, cannons roared, bonfires flared, the people shouted and sang and danced in the streets. The happy citizens were celebrating a birthday party. It was the Fourth of July and the United States was sixty years old. The country was enjoying a robust life and looking forward to a happy and vigorous future. Andrew Jackson was in the White House, serving his second term. The United States had a population of about 13,000,000 and had just welcomed Arkansas as the 25th State.

Father Neumann was anxious to go on from Rochester to Buffalo, but he had orders from Bishop Dubois to spend some time in Rochester. The Germans in Rochester attended services in the basement of St. Patrick's Church, a parish which was predominantly Irish and presided over by Father Bernard O'Reilly. The Germans wanted a church of their own and were in process of collecting funds for it. Father Joseph Prost, a Redemptorist, was on his way to minister to these people. In the meantime, Bishop Dubois wanted Father Neumann to be with them.

These German-speaking Catholics in Rochester welcomed Father Neumann as one of their own. He immediately set to work to instruct the children in catechism. To his dismay, he found the youngsters didn't speak either German or English well, but he proceeded with his instructions, doing the best he could.

In Rochester Father Neumann had his first experience with trusteeism, something which caused trouble for him and for many priests for many years. Church trustees, who were laymen, at times assumed an authority which made it difficult for the priests to administer parish affairs as they thought they should be administered. One of the trustees in Rochester stated that a new and inexperienced priest was not the type needed there. This trustee also felt that no one would go to confession to the young priest. The trustee's fears were groundless, but his words were disturbing to Father Neumann. The young priest's reaction was to ignore the atmosphere of friction and give his attention to things of the spirit, an attitude he was to pursue all his life, sometimes in the face of much more serious friction.

He administered the Sacrament of Baptism for the first time and wrote in his diary: "If the newly baptized child dies today, in the grace received from this holy sacrament, my journey to America will have been richly rewarded; yes, richly rewarded, even if in the future I accomplish nothing more." Another creature of God had been gathered into John Neumann's harvest of souls.

Father Neumann's brief stay in Rochester ended with the arrival of Father Prost. And this chance meeting between Father Prost and Father Neumann was to have an important effect on the latter's career. Father Prost made such a deep impression on Father Neumann, perhaps without realizing it, that Father Neumann felt a desire to become a Redemptorist himself. Years later Father Neumann was to realize this desire and become the Superior of the Redemptorists in the United States, the fruition of this chance meeting with a comparatively obscure but saintly and amiable priest.

Father Neumann moved on to Buffalo. He traveled once more by canalboat through the Erie Canal, "Clinton's Big Ditch," and he found Buffalo to be a thriving community. The population was 16,000 and growing fast. The canal, as an artery of commerce, helped this growth. Horse-drawn buses moved through the town and passenger cars on rails, pulled by horses, were hailed as another transportation innovation.

In Buffalo Father Neumann met Father Alexander Pax, a hard-working priest who was in ill health because of his missionary labors. His superior, Father John Nicholas Mertz, was in Europe seeking funds for the mis-

sionary work. There were four Catholic churches in the
area surrounding Buffalo, and all of them were un-
finished. Father Neumann was given his choice of any of
these churches, as his headquarters, and he selected the
church at Williamsville, eight miles outside the city.

Williamsville was a village of four houses. Father
Neumann's territory was spread out in a circle and included 400 Catholic families, most of them German.
These parishioners had come from Europe only a few
years before. They were anxious to succeed as farmers,
but they were having a hard time. They had to contend
with rough underbrush, which had to be cleared before
plowing and seeding could begin. Some of the land was
swampy in the spring and beset by mosquitoes in the
summer. The winters were harsh, with severe snow-
storms and biting cold. At times, these immigrants
lacked both money and food.

Father Neumann arranged to lodge at the home of
Jacob Philip Wirtz, one of his parishioners. The un-
finished church at Williamsville was a stone building,
without a roof. It was simply four walls, with no flooring.
There was a temporary altar and there were a few rough
benches for worshipers. A Protestant named Schmidt
had donated the land for the site, but at the time of Father Neumann's arrival the non-Catholics of the area,
particularly the young boys, were far from being neigh-
borly or friendly. The first time Father Neumann said
Mass in the church, stones were thrown over the walls
and one of them landed on the altar. The services were
frequently disturbed by a noisy clamor outside the
walls. It seemed to be a custom for some of the boys of
the neighborhood to regard such conduct as a lark. They
used to say to each other: "Let's go to the Catholic
church and have some fun!"

This was Father Neumann's first parish. One might
think a young pastor in his position would feel disheart-

ened on contemplating his future. But John Neumann came of hardy stock, physically and spiritually. He thought about this parish, in the village of Williamsville, New York, in the summer of 1836, and in his diary, together with his habitual prayerful entries, he wrote: "I am in America; I am a priest, a missionary; and I have a flock!"

CHAPTER THREE

The flock entrusted to Father Neumann included not only the Catholics of Williamsville, but also those of several other communities, in a territory which embraced 900 square miles. Niagara Falls was not far away. In a letter home, he noted that he could hear the sound of the falls as he made his missionary rounds.

His parishioners, mostly German, were intent on their farming, even under the difficult conditions they had to face. After they had cleared the land of brush and tree stumps, it was necessary to cultivate potatoes and barley for several years before they could plant wheat. This was not the dream of swift success and riches which had lured many of them to America.

While these farmers toiled on their land, the atmosphere of privation under which many of them lived was reflected in the accommodations for their spiritual life. Father Neumann visited the church at Lancaster and found it to be, in his own words, "more like a barn than a church." And yet, the way some of these immigrants clung to their faith was heartening. At North Bush the Catholics had built a log chapel, even before a priest was assigned to the area, and here they met on Sundays and holy days, to recite the rosary.

At Williamsville, Father Neumann began long-range plans for the completion of the stone church. Jacob Philip Wirtz, who had contributed generously to

24

the church fund, had also loaned the fund $400. Father Neumann persuaded Mr. Wirtz to withdraw his claim on the $400, and Mr. Wirtz agreed to do so, on condition that a memorial Mass be said for him, and for his wife, every year after their deaths. This condition was agreed upon.

As to the troublesome antics of the Williamsville boys, Father Neumann ignored them. In this attitude he reflected the feelings of Father Mertz of Buffalo: "Let us take care to make Catholics what they ought to be; the rest will take care of itself."

Writing to a friend in his native Bohemia, Father Neumann gave a word picture of how divine worship was conducted in the various centers of his parish. "The altar is usually nothing more than a table furnished with a pair of wooden candlesticks, a crucifix, a missal, two tumblers and a plate," he wrote. "From the woods around, frequently from a distance of five to ten miles, flock groups of worshipers, natives of Alsace-Lorraine, Baden, France, Ireland, etc., some on horseback, some in wagons, all in the costumes of their own nation. The more courageous among them assemble in the nearest churches on the Sundays on which they have no priest, and try to sing a hymn together. But this is difficult for some, on account of the variety of language and melody."

Even though he realized that his missionary assignment was a rigorous one for one priest, Father Neumann accepted it as a challenge and plunged zealously into his work. Because of his small stature, he was quickly labeled "the little priest" by people in the area. He became a familiar sight, walking on foot most of the time and carrying on his back a pack which contained his vestments and other necessities for saying Mass and administering the sacraments.

Forests, dense woods and swamps covered most of

his mission territory. Through the heat of summer and
the cold of winter he made his rounds. His friend, Father
Pax of Buffalo, tried to get him to ease up in his strenu-
ous efforts, but such a course was foreign to Father Neumann's temperament. "I'm a strong Bohemian mountain boy," he said cheerfully and continued his arduous
routine, saying Mass, hearing confessions, teaching catechism, baptizing, marrying and doing any pastoral
chore which presented itself in his far-flung domain.

At Williamsville, in addition to his parish duties, he
took on the work of conducting a school for the children
of that area. He gave two hours in the morning and two
hours in the afternoon to this activity. His nearest mission post was a two-hour journey from Williamsville and
the farthest away was a twelve-hour journey. When he
visited the mission posts, he returned as quickly as possible.

"Many of our Catholics are in extreme poverty,"
Father Neumann wrote to a friend at home. "They live
in miserable shanties, some of which have not even the
luxury of a window. As a general thing, chairs and bed-
steads are unknown. I have seen the dying stretched on a
bundle of straw or moss. To hear their confessions and
prepare them for the sacraments, I have to seat myself
by their side on the ground."

One night, as Father Neumann was returning home
on foot after a sick call, he was caught in a severe thunderstorm. He lost his way in the pitch blackness of a
swampy terrain. Then he saw a dim light, which came
from a cabin. He rapped on the door, and a child's
frightened voice answered: "We let no one in at night."

Father Neumann continued his rapping. He plead-
ed for shelter and the little girl finally let him in. Her father lay in a corner of the cabin, with only some moss between him and the ground. He appeared to be ill. He
told Father Neumann somewhat despondently that his

wife and his other children had died recently. He and the little girl who had let Father Neumann in were the only members of the family surviving. Father Neumann gave the man some altar wine from his pack and this revived his spirits. He said he was happy to see a priest and he made his confession.

Father Neumann stayed at the cabin until the next day and when he left the man seemed much improved in his whole outlook. The young priest was happy in the thought that, in a seemingly random way, out of a thunderstorm, he had made contact with two members of his flock whom he otherwise might not have known.

On another occasion, Father Neumann was walking through the woods and his feet, blistered by miles of traveling, became very painful. He sat under a tree to rest. Within a matter of minutes, he was surrounded by a band of roving Indians. Similar groups had robbed lonely travelers, and the young priest expected they would take whatever of his possessions appealed to them. But the Indians recognized Father Neumann as "a black gown," a man to be aided and treated with respect. Seeing that his feet were giving him trouble, they spread a blanket on the ground, placed "the little priest" on it, and carried him to his destination.

Father Neumann sometimes made his missionary journeys in a wagon. Returning home in his wagon one day, after baptizing a child, he was suddenly pitched onto the road at a sharp turn. His left arm was badly hurt and there was a danger that it would have to be amputated. The arm healed eventually, but for a period of two weeks he was unable to say Mass.

Through all of these happenings, Father Neumann went about his pastoral work in routine fashion, disregarding the hardships and trying to minister to his people as he might in a city parish. "My first sermon was well received," he noted in his diary after first coming to

Williamsville. "I ascribe its success to the intercession of
the Blessed Virgin Mary, to whom I have promised to introduce among the children the Confraternity of the
Most Blessed Sacrament."

After he had said Mass at one of his stations he
would gather the children together for catechism instruction, a duty which was for him a labor of love. The
children began to anticipate these catechism classes
with eager delight. They would gather around the young
priest and some might even thrust their hands into his
coat pockets, seeking candy or other gifts which he
usually had for them. He not only taught them Christian
Doctrine, but also reading, writing and arithmetic. And
he rewarded the best students with medals, rosaries and
holy pictures.

In going about his duties, Father Neumann found
that he, as pastor, was living in poverty as austere as
that of his parishioners. A resident of the mission area
had assured Bishop Dubois that the new pastor would
have an income of about $300 a year, but this never ma-
terialized. Many of Father Neumann's people, in their
European homeland, had become accustomed to the
fact that the government paid the salaries of the priests,
and so the duty of supporting their church and pastor in
America was distasteful to them. So Father Neumann
went his way, utilizing the money received for the best
interests of his missions. It was his nature to think of
himself last. In fact, along about the time he began to
handle parish funds, he became alarmed lest he might
get greedy, and he took a vow of poverty, thereafter re-
stricting himself to the bare necessities. Some of his
more solicitous parishioners wondered at times if he had
enough to eat. His general attitude about such temporal
things was revealed in a letter to a friend in which he
said: "If you want to be a missionary, you have to love
poverty."

One sect in Father Neumann's territory exhibited great zeal in trying to make converts. They visited the homes of people, carrying Bibles, ready to exhort and argue. They succeeded in making some converts to their sect among Father Neumann's people and he was worried about their activities.

One Sunday he was walking through deep snow, en route to one of his churches, when a horse-drawn sleigh passed him. It stopped and he was invited to get in. The man driving the sleigh was the minister of the zealous sect who sought to convert Father Neumann's parishioners. The minister offered to give Father Neumann a lift on his journey.

Father Neumann gratefully accepted the invitation, but was embarrassed when his host tried to convince him that he should join the minister's sect. The outcome of the meeting was that Father Neumann and the minister agreed to meet in a public debate on the respective merits of their religions.

The event attracted wide attention in the area. It was decided to have an impartial chairman of the debate, and this condition was fulfilled perfectly when a well-known lawyer, who said he had no religion, accepted the chairmanship. The debate was staged with some ceremony and members of Father Neumann's parish, together with members of the minister's sect, gathered at a public meeting place.

The debate revolved around the Bible, its history and its sources. Father Neumann, having learned this subject well in his seminary days, was able to confound his opponent very easily. The young priest was talented in this area where minds clashed. With rapier-like thrusts, backed by his erudition, he was able to rout his opponent with no great effort. Henceforth, members of the minister's sect were not quite so zealous in seeking converts among the Catholics. And the label of "the lit-

tle priest," which was used by some members of this sect
with scorn, was used now in tones of respect, with over-
tones of awe.

Father Neumann was by nature quiet and retiring.
He had no urge to take part in the debate, except that
the issue had been forced upon him. At another time,
confronted by an argumentative individual, he sought
refuge in silence, and this infuriated his antagonist. The
man shouted arguments at him in a public place. The
young priest walked on as if he didn't hear them. The
man, in a rage, drew a gun and yelled: "You damned
priest, if you don't turn around and talk with me, I'll
shoot you!" Father Neumann didn't turn around. The
man didn't shoot. Father Neumann had shown courage
and self-control, but the impression he made on his ad-
versary was probably that of an austere cleric who felt
himself superior to his fellowman.

Entries in his diary reveal his true attitude. "Give
me an ever-increasing love for Thy redeemed ones," he
wrote, "that I may labor at their salvation in wisdom,
patience and holiness. Grant that not one of those whom
Thou hast confided to me be lost through my fault."
And again: "Lord, teach me how to live, and, if needs be
to die, for my people, that they may all be saved, that
they may all love and praise Thee in eternity, that they
may love Thy dear Mother!"

After Father Neumann had lived in Williamsville
for about six months he moved his headquarters to
North Bush. He was given free lodging by one of his parishioners, a man named John Schmidt. He had to walk
a mile and a half to the church each morning to say
Mass, but he accepted this pattern as part of his work.
The parishioners at North Bush presented him with a
five-acre tract of land, where he could build a rectory
and have a vegetable garden. He worked on the building
of the house himself, aided by his friendly people, and at

length he was able to move into his new home. It was only a log cabin of two rooms. The door at the entrance was so low that a tall man had to stoop to enter; it was probably built with Father Neumann's height of five feet four inches in mind. For furniture he had only a few chairs. But this home of his own was a great comfort to the young pastor. Here he could cook his own meals, when he took time out from his work to prepare a meal. Here he had his own precious books, his little library. And, not far away was the church, where he could make frequent visits to the Blessed Sacrament.

Bishop Dubois made an official visitation to North Bush and the missionary territory. He was pleased with Father Neumann's work and told him so. The young priest was heartened by this praise. He was always telling himself that he was slothful, because he didn't accomplish all that he saw to be accomplished in his vast mission field.

The financial panic of 1837 descended upon the country and Father Neumann's people were hard hit. In the large cities of the country, giant business enterprises collapsed. The cancer of depression reached into every corner of the nation. The farmers of Father Neumann's area, already hard-pressed, were drawn further into the whirlpool of poverty. Some of them saw practically no money during the whole year. They had to resort to bartering their crops for what they needed. Money could not be borrowed, even if a prospective borrower offered twenty percent interest.

Father Neumann was given food, gifts of corn and potatoes, by his parishioners. They also gave him clothing now and then and these things he accepted gratefully. News from home at about this time was a source of spiritual joy. His sister Joan had become a nun in the order of the Sisters of Charity of St. Charles Borromeo.

As he contemplated his mission territory, Father

Neumann often thought of ways and means by which more missionaries could be brought to this area from Europe. Naturally, he thought of ways in which priests could be brought from his native Bohemia. At one time he sought to have a mission-house established in Bohemia, for the purpose of serving America. At another time he planned to have a seminary established in the Buffalo area, for German-speaking priests who would come from Europe. He obtained permission from New York diocesan authorities to secure new priests through his European connections.

"It is not necessary for them to speak English or French," he wrote eagerly. "They can easily learn both languages in this country."

Again, he penned the hopeful lines: "If my petition meets, as I hope it will, a favorable response, you would oblige me by letting me know at once. With the names of the aspirants, state also the time of their setting out for America."

He had some correspondence with a friend of his seminary days: "The idea of the American missions was at that time so closely interwoven with our one great thought, the service of God and our neighbor, that any other road leading thereto, how well-known or secure soever it might be, appeared to us foreign and distasteful," he reminded his friend. "You still sigh, if I may credit your own words, for America and your friend of bygone days. Why, then, do you not come?"

Nobody came.

Father Neumann was destined to serve out these missionary years alone.

CHAPTER FOUR

As Father Neumann continued with his busy schedule, some of his parishioners gave him a horse, to help him make his rounds. He was thankful for the gift, but he must have had serious misgivings about his ability to make use of it. Father Neumann was no horseman and he knew it.

In the early stages of his acquaintanceship with his steed, he would often mount by leading the horse to a fence, where he could literally climb aboard. The horse seemed to sense the amateur qualities of his rider and didn't make things any easier for the young priest. The horse would sometimes trot along very close to a fence, leaving Father Neumann with the choice of getting a leg scraped or dismounting. Again, the horse would stop dead in the middle of a muddy road. If Father Neumann wanted to go further, he would have to dismount and lead the animal, walking through the mud until the horse decided he would again be obedient and helpful.

Although he was not an experienced horseman, Father Neumann did manage to master his steed well enough so that it eventually became a great help to him as he traveled to his mission stations. The animal, however, never lost its talent for being a nuisance, often at the most unexpected times and in the most unexpected ways.

The young priest, a keen student of botany ever

since his school days, was fascinated by the unusual
floral specimens he saw as he traveled through his missionary territory. One day, riding his horse, he noticed
some rare flowers growing by the roadside. He stopped
his horse and dismounted. The beast seemed to be in a
friendly mood and stood quietly by, while Father Neumann gathered the flowers.

They would be wonderful to send to botanist friends
in Bohemia, the young priest thought as he walked back
to his horse. He was holding the precious flowers in his
hand, and admiring the way they looked in the bright
sunlight, when the horse suddenly stretched his neck,
seized the flowers in his teeth, and devoured them!

Father Neumann often told this story on himself in
after years. He appreciated the humor of it, which was
his reason for telling it, but he also added the serious
words: "That was the sacrifice God wanted from me at
that moment."

In his experiences with his horse, Father Neumann
sometimes became the object of ridicule from people of
the area. This didn't disturb him; he was too intent on
his work. But such things may have served, like other incidents in his missionary life, to give observers a false
impression of the young priest and what he was like in
his real self, behind the facade of his outward appearance and conduct. Some observers might have thought
he was timid, vacillating and easily pushed around.

During the time he lived in Williamsville, in the
home of Mr. Wirtz, a servant girl boarded there. Gossips
soon began to circulate stories. The mildest thing they
said was that the young priest should not board in the
same house with a young girl. The gossip was begun by a
neighbor of Mr. Wirtz, who was jealous because the pastor did not board with him. There was a certain prestige
attached to having Father Neumann as a boarder, and
apparently there were status seekers in parish affairs in

those days, just as there are today. The gossip came to a
climax when a group of trustees met and dispatched a
messenger to Father Neumann, asking him to appear
before them. When Father Neumann obeyed the summons, the trustees told him of the gossip. His reaction
was to quietly disavow any misconduct. The trustees accepted his mild protestations. But some of his parishioners, no doubt, would probably have been better satisfied,
and better entertained, by verbal fireworks. They probably didn't realize that it was not in Father Neumann's
character to be explosive and to engage in long drawn-
out, bombastic talk.

Later, thinking over the effects the gossip might
have, Father Neumann decided to move to North Bush.
This may have been accepted by some of his people as
evidence that he could be maneuvered and swayed by
pressure groups among his parishioners.

This was not true and there were occasions when he
demonstrated clearly that he could be as firm and unyielding as the situation demanded. The crux of the
matter was that he could be firm and unyielding only
when the situation demanded it in his own judgment,
and not in the judgment of others.

One of the things that caused the young priest concern, in relation to the spiritual welfare of his flock, was
the presence of saloons in his mission territory. Although
he hardly ever drank anything alcoholic himself, he had
no objection to drinking in moderation. What worried
him was the fact that some of his people drank in a way
far from moderate, and spent money for liquor which
they could better use for the necessities of life. Also, he
noticed that a very busy saloon seemed always to
operate not far from each of his churches, as though further to hinder him when he sought to make the churches
quiet havens where his parishioners could find spiritual
peace.

At one of his mission stations, he heard that the parishioners were planning to hold a gala dance on a forthcoming holy day. The affair, elaborate in its planning and involving most of his parishioners in that area, was to be held in a saloon near the church. This, in Father Neumann's judgment, was something that demanded his firmness.

In his sermon on the Sunday before the holy day, he spoke out against holding the dance. To make it clear how he felt, he told his people he would no longer serve them if they persisted in their plans. The parishioners continued preparations for the dance, apparently with the thought that "the little priest" was very easygoing and would never do anything drastic.

After Mass on the holy day, with the saloon ready for the gala dance and the parishioners ready too, a wagon drove up to Father Neumann's residence. The driver told inquirers that he had been hired to take Father Neumann's belongings away.

"You must have offended him," the driver said. "He's going to leave you."

The news spread and a crowd gathered. The people, alarmed, were suddenly struck with the thought that maybe Father Neumann had meant what he said. They were sure of it a few minutes later when the young priest appeared. He reminded them that he had previously made his position clear. The people had chosen their course. And Father Neumann had chosen his.

"I will no longer be your pastor," he told them.

The people were shocked into facing reality. They pleaded with Father Neumann not to leave. They promised to call off the dance. He agreed to stay on this condition and the dance was not held. Thereafter, when Father Neumann spoke his mind, in his usual mild tones, his people had good reason to believe that he meant what he said.

As the weeks and months went by, Father Neumann continued to serve his mission territory. He faced the fact that none of his friends of seminary days were going to join him, and that no other plans promised any help, in the matter of bringing more priests to the area. So he went his rounds, resigned to the situation. But, thinking back to his home and family in Bohemia, as he often did, he hit upon the idea that maybe his brother Wenceslaus would like to join him. The more he thought about it, the more he was convinced that Wenceslaus could be of great help to him. And, being human, he yearned for the companionship of someone he felt close to, someone who could tell him, not by letter but by word of mouth, how everything and everybody was in the little two-story brick house in the faraway village of Prachatitz.

He wrote home, suggesting that Wenceslaus join him. He wrote more than once, pleading that his younger brother make the trip. Wenceslaus was eager to go. His parents had no serious objections, although his father could have insisted, understandably, that he needed Wenceslaus to help him in his business.

But there were no serious objections, and so Wenceslaus set sail for America, traveling on an American clipper, the type of sailing vessel which was at that time the pride of the Atlantic. Father Neumann had sent Wenceslaus explicit directions on how to proceed from New York to his mission territory. It was a happy day, September 25, 1839, when the two brothers were reunited.

Wenceslaus threw himself into the mission activities, doing anything and everything he could, as a layman, to help his brother. One important contribution Wenceslaus made was to act as cook for Father Neumann. The young priest was somewhat careless in the matter of eating regularly and, because of his abstemious nature, he sometimes seemed not to care whether he ate or not. Among the resolutions he made after his arrival in missionary territory, Father Neumann, as a matter of self-denial, put himself on a schedule of eating only two meals a day. Wenceslaus could at least be sure that the two meals were well prepared.

Wenceslaus also kept the little log cabin rectory spotlessly clean, relieving his brother of such chores. And Wenceslaus helped, too, in teaching the classes Father Neumann conducted for the children in his parishes.

Most importantly, Wenceslaus brought to his brother a little bit of home. Listening to Wenceslaus and his reports on family and friends, Father Neumann felt transported, even if only briefly, back to his native village. He could see his father, supervising the men who worked for him as stocking-makers. He could see his mother, sitting beside an open window, distributing food to the poor, a weekly custom she observed for years. He could see the shortcut through the village square, which he used to take on his way to school. And he could see his sisters, Catherine, Veronica, Louise and Joan. True, Joan was in the convent now, and he and Wenceslaus were in America, but Father Neumann saw the family dinner table with everybody seated at it, as it used to be in his childhood, without the empty chairs.

Wenceslaus was of great help to Father Neumann in working on the building of new churches. Two such buildings were being constructed in the mission territory, together with a log cabin for each parish priest. It was Father Neumann's ideal to prepare each of the church properties for the day when they would be separate parishes, each with its own pastor.

With Wenceslaus by his side, one might think that Father Neumann would enjoy a measure of contentment, while he worked in the vast expanses of his mission territory. But he was far from content. He felt that he lacked zeal in his work, at the very time he was burning himself out to perform his priestly duties. His smallest failures seemed to him to be great defects.

Travail of soul afflicted him. Always a prayerful man, he now experienced periods of spiritual aridity in which he was not able to find consolation in his prayers and meditations. This anguish reached a point where he felt unworthy of his calling and he even thought of going away.

"In my faint-heartedness, I indulged wild dreams," he wrote in his journal. "To escape the terrible responsibility resting upon me, I sometimes thought of abandoning my flock, of fleeing to some distant solitude where I might lead a hidden, penitential life, or hire myself as a laborer in the fields. The fear of creating suspicion in the minds of the faithful, and of affording the enemies of our holy religion occasion to blaspheme, alone prevented my carrying out this project."

His peace of soul eventually was restored, but his physical health was in decline. The "strong Bohemian mountain boy" who had brushed aside the urging of his friend, Father Pax, to take things a bit easier, knew of only one way to serve his God and his people, and that was to give his all. In the summer of 1840 he suffered a physical breakdown.

Intermittent fever afflicted him with violent and weakening attacks. He was unable to perform his parish duties and had to take to his bed. Wenceslaus gave him tender care and attention, but for three months Father Neumann was obliged to rest and recuperate. During this time, no one among his parishioners was in need of a priest for a sick call and the young priest interpreted this gratefully as a gift of God to him and his people.

During his convalescence he visited Father Pax in Buffalo. He confided to Father Pax, who was his confessor, that he would like to become a Redemptorist. Father Pax approved of this step.

This was no sudden thought on the part of Father Neumann. He had felt at various times in the past that his vocation was to be a member of a religious order. He had a strong desire to live in community with other priests. Regarding the Redemptorists, he had been impressed, when he first visited Rochester in 1836, by the saintliness and sincerity of Father Prost. Subsequently, in 1838, when he again visited Rochester to substitute for Father Prost during the latter's absence, he was impressed by the fact that there was a spirit of piety among the German Catholics of Rochester which was not in evidence when he first ministered to them. Father Neumann attributed this to the Redemptorists and it increased his desire to become a member of that order.

Returning to his missions, Father Neumann made plans to join the Redemptorists. "I think this is the best thing I can do for the security of my salvation," he wrote to his parents. "The constant supervision of religious supervisors and the good example of fellow religious . . . spur one to lead a life more pleasing to God than one can lead in the world."

He made formal application to the Redemptorists and his application was accepted. New York diocesan authorities were reluctant to have Father Neumann leave the missionary territory he served so diligently, but they gave their consent. The young priest packed his personal belongings and Wenceslaus set out to collect various possessions of Father Neumann's, at the mission stations, to be delivered to him later.

Leaving his missionary territory, Father Neumann probably felt he had not achieved any great results in his four years of labor. If he could have looked forward through the years, he would have felt differently. Today, Catholic parishes dot the whole area of his mission field and many Catholics of the region proudly trace their ancestry back to the pioneer settlers who, under the young priest's guidance, kept alive the heritage of faith.

The village of North Bush is no more, but in its place is the thriving community of Kenmore. Serving in place of the once roofless church in Williamsville is the church of Ss. Peter and Paul. Each year in this church a memorial Mass is said for Mr. Wirtz and another for his wife. In Williamsville, not far from the spot where Father Neumann taught catechism to the children stands an imposing building, the Neumann High School.

But these developments were far in the future on the day in early October, 1840, when Father Neumann left North Bush for Buffalo, on the first step of his journey to new fields.

CHAPTER FIVE

Biting winds whipped the lake waters as a small steamer chugged through the night, en route from Buffalo to Erie.

The little ship was crowded with 400 immigrants. They had only recently arrived in New York. Now they were again on the move, to become part of pioneer America as it spread into cities, farms and plains. So many passengers had come aboard the ship that, for many, there was "standing room only." They seemed not to mind, at this stage of the voyage. They were hardy peasants, physically strong and buoyed up by their dreams of wealth and happiness in America.

Father Neumann stood on the deck of the little ship, among the standees. He was on his way to the Redemptorist headquarters in Pittsburgh. Looking over the ship's rail, he watched the choppy waters. He knew the weather of the region well enough to realize that a storm was brewing. The wind was rising. Lake Erie was being churned into a fury.

The young priest studied his fellow passengers. Seeing them in this setting, he was reminded of his long voyage to America, four years ago. The passengers were the same types as those who had sailed with him on the *Europa*. Family groups huddled together, sheltering themselves as best they could from the raw winds. They wore shawls, heavy coats and the colorful costumes of their homelands. They seemed subdued, speaking only among themselves. Children clung tearfully to their mothers as the ship bobbed and tossed in the mounting waves. Older folks stood silent, quietly resigned to whatever the elements had in store.

All through the night the little ship rose and fell in the heaving seas. Children cried. Their mothers comforted them. Nobody rested. Nobody slept. At dawn, the passengers looked to see where they were. They were due to dock in Erie that morning. They saw land not far away, but it was the city of Buffalo, which they had left at 9 o'clock the night before. They had made practically no progress.

The little steamer docked at Buffalo and took on more coal, then set out again, but again the rough waters toyed with it, holding it back. A passing vessel gave the steamer more coal. It battled bravely on, through the second night. Near Erie, the captain feared it would be grounded on a sandbar. He changed his course, waiting for the storm to subside. Finally, he brought the little ship into Erie. It had taken more than 50 hours to make a journey which, in good weather, was a simple overnight trip.

The passengers, freed from their fears, went on their way. They were hungry, having taken no provisions aboard, but they were happy. The storm was over. They were nearer to their various destinations, nearer to the time when they could begin to work and prosper as they dreamed they would when they left the shores of Europe, long weeks before.

Father Neumann visited a Franciscan priest in Erie. The next day, rested and refreshed, he boarded a stagecoach. Two days later, he arrived in Pittsburgh.

Pittsburgh in 1840 had a population of 50,000. It was a bustling community, already showing signs of developing into a great industrial city. The country was in the midst of a presidential election campaign. President Martin Van Buren was running for re-election against William Henry Harrison. This was the campaign in which the voters heard the slogan: "Tippecanoe and Tyler too." Tyler was running with Harrison as the candidate for Vice President and the slogan reminded voters that Harrison was the hero of the battle of Tippecanoe. Harrison was to win the election. The popular vote was close, 1,275,017 to 1,128,702, but the electoral votes totaled 234 for Harrison against 60 for Van Buren. President Harrison died after serving only one month in office and was succeeded by the Vice President, John Tyler.

But matters of politics were far from Father Neumann's mind when he arrived in Pittsburgh on October 18, 1840. It was a Sunday. He reported at the Redemptorist headquarters and his first duty was to sing a High Mass and preach a sermon. This he did in a building which had once been a factory and was known as "The Factory Church."

The Pittsburgh headquarters of the Redemptorists was one of four foundations which the order had established in this country. Others were in Baltimore, Rochester, and Norwalk, Ohio. They were hardy men of God, these pioneer Redemptorists. They were followers of St. Alphonsus Liguori, who founded the order in Naples in 1732. It was the plan of the founder to one day send Redemptorists to America, but this did not happen until 1832 when Venerable Father Joseph Passerat, then Superior of the order, sent three priests and three Brothers to this country, in response to a request from Church authorities in Ohio. These Redemptorists spoke German, which made them especially welcome to German Catholic immigrants. They suffered many privations. The annals of the order tell of Redemptorist Fathers battling cholera outbreaks in the midwest and bringing spiritual comfort to settlers spread over a wide expanse.

The Diocese of Ohio at that time embraced the whole state of Ohio and areas which later were part of the states of Wisconsin and Michigan.

Father Passerat had predicted in 1836 that the order, officially known as the Congregation of the Most Holy Redeemer, would have its first official foundation in America in the year St. Alphonsus was canonized. St. Alphonsus was canonized three years later, in 1839.

In that year, a farmer named Adelmann, who lived near Pittsburgh, had occasion to visit Norwalk, Ohio. He was impressed by the way the Redemptorists ministered to the Catholics of the area and he urged Father Prost, who was serving there, to send Redemptorists to the German Catholics of Pittsburgh. Father Prost explained that they could not go into a diocese without invitation from the bishop.

This was answer enough for Mr. Adelmann. He brought his request to the attention of Bishop Francis Patrick Kenrick of Philadelphia, whose diocese included Pittsburgh, and within three weeks Father Prost had a letter from Bishop Kenrick, inviting the Redemptorists to Pittsburgh.

Father Prost surveyed the situation in Pittsburgh and learned that in a group of German Catholics there had been serious friction between the trustees and the clergy. Prior to Father Prost's coming, attempts had been made to restore harmony. Some of the people attended St. Patrick's Church. Others attended services in the factory building. But even this did not restore peace. When Father Prost arrived on the scene, the German Catholics had been without a pastor for weeks.

Father Prost talked with some of the disputants and succeeded in calming their quarrelsomeness. The factory building, which previously had been rented, was purchased and became St. Philomena's Church, though it continued to be referred to by many as "The Factory

Church." There was enough room in the building for living quarters for priests. And so, out of friction and strife, came the fulfillment of Father Passerat's prediction. The Redemptorists, in the year of St. Alphonsus' canonization, had their first house in the new world. Up to that time, though working zealously in America, they had no official house of their own.

When Father Neumann came on the scene a year later to begin his novitiate, he was welcomed by Father Francis Tschenhens, who was in charge of St. Philomena's. Father Prost, now Superior of the order in America, had decided that Father Neumann should spend his year as a novice under Father Tschenhens' direction.

But, almost at once, circumstances changed these plans. Father Tschenhens had to go to Baltimore, to be assistant at St. John's, as the work was too much for the one priest stationed there. This left Father Neumann at St. Philomena's with Father Peter Czackert. The latter was absent a great deal, visiting outlying missions. Father Neumann had been looking forward to a year of prayer, meditation and spiritual direction, but this was not to be. He had to serve as parish priest and at the same time be his own Novice Master and his own Superior.

"There was no novitiate in America at that time, and no Novice Master, but an overwhelming amount of work to be dispatched," Father Neumann wrote later of this period. "I daily made two meditations and two examens of conscience with the community, spiritual reading in private, and a visit to the Blessed Sacrament. I recited the Rosary, also, and that was all."

About a month after his coming to Pittsburgh, Father Neumann welcomed his brother Wenceslaus, who brought the young priest's belongings which had been left at mission stations in his former territory. Father

Neumann was happy to see his brother again. He recalled how Wenceslaus, when told of his plan to join the Redemptorists, had said: "I'll go with you." Father Neumann had been very pleased at this. Wenceslaus served with the Redemptorists as a zealous and humble lay Brother until his death more than fifty years later.

Adjusting as best he could to the strange terms of his novitiate, Father Neumann performed parish duties. He had not forgotten his resolution of years ago, never to waste a minute. He taught catechism, he preached, he went on sick calls, he baptized. When Father Czackert was away, Father Neumann, in the unusual position of being both a novice and an ordained priest, performed whatever priestly duties were required.

On November 30, 1840, Father Prost vested Father Neumann in the habit of the Redemptorist Order. The ceremony took place in St. Philomena's after a High Mass. It was a solemn occasion, somewhat marred by the fact that there was no official copy of the ritual for investiture at hand. Several copies were kept in New York, but these had been destroyed in a fire. So Father Prost had to trust to memory in conducting the investiture.

Even though the ceremony may have lacked some of the grandeur of the usual carefully phrased questions, answers and prayers, Father Neumann was now officially vested in the Redemptorist habit. The making of his vows was scheduled for about a year ahead, at the conclusion of his period as a novice.

So he plunged into his work with renewed energy. He and Father Czackert rode on horseback to neighboring towns and villages and Father Neumann was grateful for his earlier experience as a horseman. But he was not to enjoy this comparative calm for long. In May of 1841 he was moved to St. John's in Baltimore. Several more Redemptorists had arrived from Europe and more space was needed in the Pittsburgh house. After three days in Baltimore, he was sent to New York, to help out at St. Nicholas Church, where he had said his first Mass five years before. He was pleased to be once more at St. Nicholas', but two weeks later he was ordered to Rochester, to continue his novitiate under Father Tschenhens, and two months after that he was dispatched to Buffalo, to help out his friend, Father Pax, who was ill. Soon afterwards, he was sent to the log cabin rectory in Norwalk, Ohio.

During this moving about, Father Neumann became worried about his position in the order. He was upset by the nagging thought that perhaps he was being sent here and there because, among his own brethren, he was not wanted!

Father Prost, knowing his sensitive and diffident nature, sensed what was bothering him and wrote in a letter: "Do not think that you are a burden. On the contrary, you are universally loved and cherished." But Father Tschenhens told him more than once, perhaps to test his determination: "You had better return to your former missions. You will never persevere with us."

Gnawing doubts began to attack Father Neumann's peace of mind. Out of them came the thought that perhaps, after all, he should not become a Redemptorist. His own basic attitude in this period of turmoil is clearly revealed in his diary.

"O my God," he wrote, "You know my blindness! Do not permit that I alone must choose; arrange the influences that bear upon me so that if it pleases You, no doubt may remain about my vocation or lack of vocation. But if, my Lord, it is Your Will that I remain in doubt and be uneasy, then may Your Will be done until death! You are the supreme, all-knowing and good God. I am Yours; save me!"

Father Neumann was ordered to go from Norwalk to

Baltimore, to conclude his novitiate, and to give missions along the way. He took a stagecoach to Canton, Ohio, where his troubled spirits received a severe jolt. He heard a rumor that the Redemptorists were about to be dissolved in this country.

The rumor was false, but Father Neumann had no way of determining this at the time. The Bishop of Cincinnati urged him to join that diocese. Father Neumann, though harassed by this new torment, declined the bishop's invitation.

He did agree to the bishop's request that he visit Randolph, Ohio, and try to quiet two quarrelsome factions among the parishioners. On going to Randolph he found that this was no minor quarrel. One of the embittered factions had burned down the parish church!

Father Neumann gave a mission at Randolph. For ten days he preached twice a day. He instructed the children in catechism and every evening the rosary was recited by the congregation. Even though the weather was bitterly cold, the people responded. Father Neumann heard the confessions of hundreds. The people thronged to receive Communion. Peace came again to the parish. But not to Father Neumann.

He moved on toward Baltimore and his hour of decision. He became sick on the lurching stagecoach and left it near Steubenville, Ohio. He spent two days recuperating in the home of strangers. These people belonged to no organized religious group, but they extended the hand of charity to a wayfarer, physically ill and spiritually distraught.

When he felt well again, Father Neumann continued his journey. Though physically able to perform his priestly duties, his mind was not at rest. Years later, writing about the trials and temptations novices experience, Father Neumann revealed that, despite the odd pattern of his own novitiate, he was keenly aware of them.

"This novice imagines himself deficient in physical strength," he wrote. "Another deludes himself with the notion that things would go more smoothly in another order, or that he could possibly do more good for the honor of God while living in the world. Sadness and melancholy seize upon some while others are beset by a love of their own ease. Some are attacked with homesickness, or other temptations born of self-will, disgust for prayer, want of confidence in their superiors, and so forth. The temptations of the soul are doubtless as numerous as the disorders of the body, but to remain steadfast and to persevere in all this turmoil of spirit, there is no better remedy than prayer to the Blessed Virgin for the grace of perseverance. At the same time, immediate disclosure of the temptation to one's director is absolutely necessary."

When he came to Baltimore, Father Neumann was given several weeks to spend in prayer and quiet. This brought balm to his troubled soul. Struggling through doubt and worry, he began to see things more clearly. As the concluding act of his novitiate, he made a spiritual retreat and now his uncertainty was resolved. On January 16, 1842, he made his profession of vows and was received into the Congregation of the Most Holy Redeemer.

Father Neumann was the first Redemptorist to be received into the order in the United States. The official chronicler, apparently unable to resist the temptation to be a punster, wrote into the annals: "A new man has entered the Congregation."

CHAPTER SIX

The "new man" was very happy to be a member of the Congregation. "I now belong to it body and soul," he wrote to his parents. "The mutual bodily and spiritual help, edification and good example, which one has around him till his death in such a spiritual society, makes my life and my office a great deal easier for me."

Very quickly he became absorbed in work. Not only parish duties, but missionary visits to outlying sections were part of his labors. All of the German Catholics of Maryland were now under the Redemptorists' care. Working out of Baltimore, Father Neumann went to various sections of the missionary territory.

This was work with which he was familiar, being similar to his missionary duties in the Buffalo area. In New York, he had become known as "the little priest." In Maryland, he quickly became known as "the little Redemptorist." His physical stature was, of course, the same, a meager five feet, four inches. His manner was pretty much the same; he was still inclined to be shy and quite often he did not make a good first impression on people he met. His deep-set eyes were the same, penetrating, and reflecting his concentration on any task at hand.

And so, as a Redemptorist, Father Neumann went about the day-to-day business of gleaning his harvest of souls. He traveled by canalboat and stagecoach, on

horseback and on foot. In some mission areas months
would go by between his visits, because of the vast expanse to be covered and the need for more priests. "The
few we have are sadly out of proportion with the ever-
increasing wants of the faithful," he wrote on the subject. "There are Catholics who have not been to confession for many years, and there are young persons of nineteen or twenty who have nothing of Catholicity about
them saving their baptism — and all this from the want
of priests. The longer this need continues, the more difficult it will be to reanimate faith and the fear of God."

The German Catholics living outside of the cities
and towns were objects of special concern to the Redemptorists. "Most of them arrive in their new homes
without money or goods," Father Alexander Czvit-
kovicz, who succeeded Father Prost as the Superior of
the order in America, said of them. "They give little
thought to their religion or priests, for they live scattered
in the forests or in the existing German settlements,
where they eke out a miserable existence. In consequence of their isolation and poverty they drift into a
state of religious indifferentism, or, as frequently hap-
pens, fall victims to the proselytizing of heretical sects.
This deplorable effect of emigration from Europe is a
historical fact."

Father Neumann was officially assigned as an assistant at St. James Church in Baltimore. In addition to
his mission assignments, he worked with another priest,
Father Fay, in performing parish duties. There were the
customary matters of saying Mass and administering
the sacraments and teaching catechism to the children.
And there were always a number of adults, sometimes as
many as thirty, under instruction to become converts to
the faith. In spite of their worries about temporal matters, such as earning their livelihood in a strange land,
these immigrants in Baltimore found time to be con-

cerned also with their spiritual welfare. Almost every Sunday there were converts to be baptized.

In performing his priestly duties, both in St. James parish and in the mission field, Father Neumann had a keen understanding of the people, born of experience and his intense interest in bringing them spiritual peace and comfort. He knew their yearnings, their motivations, their faults, their good deeds, their plans and their dreams. Writing to a friend in Europe, he said of these immigrants: "That the evils existing among our people are very great is, indeed, only too true, and the reason of [*sic*] this is that many of them are mere adventurers, restless fanatics, sighing for what they call liberty; and some there are who have but narrowly escaped the outstretched arms of justice."

But, though he could make this forthright appraisal, his attitude, even toward criminals, was a charitable one. In Baltimore during Father Neumann's service there, a man was sentenced to be hanged for murder. The man had been married twice and had been tried and convicted on charges of killing both wives. The day of the hanging, January 12, 1844, was turned into something of a gala occasion by the public. A great crowd gathered before the platform where the execution was to take place.

The people were chattering away, as though waiting impatiently to see an entertaining spectacle. But the hum of their voices ceased and a hush fell over the crowd as the murderer took his place on the scaffold. Beside him stood Father Neumann. His presence seemed to destroy the thrill the crowd had anticipated. Many seemed subdued when they saw "the little Redemptorist." He remained at the condemned man's side until the trap was sprung and the sentence of death was carried out. He had not come to enjoy any macabre thrills, but simply to extend spiritual comfort to a repentant sinner.

In March of 1844, Father Neumann was made pastor of St. Philomena's in Pittsburgh. He returned to the parish where he had begun his novitiate. There had been some changes since that time.

Pittsburgh now had its own diocese, separate from Philadelphia. It embraced, approximately, the western half of the state. Bishop Michael O'Connor had only twenty-one priests to serve the 45,000 Catholics of the diocese, an area which included a total population of 800,000.

At St. Philomena's a new church was being built. The factory building had been torn down and a temporary church and school had been erected. Some time before Father Neumann's arrival as pastor, the trustee system had generated serious trouble. Some of the parishioners felt that, under this system, they should have a voice in every matter connected with the church. Some of them made claims on the church property. Father Alexander, the Redemptorist Superior in America at the time, found it necessary to call a meeting of the parishioners and to state frankly that, if some of them persisted in contesting the right of the order to the church property, the Redemptorists would leave Pittsburgh. The meeting was a hectic one. Arguments were being voiced for and against the trustee system when Jacob Schneider, original owner of the "Factory Church" property, arose and settled the dispute with blunt words.

"This is none of your affair, therefore be silent," he told the dissenting parishioners. "No one has a right to a word on the subject. All this property was once mine. I sold it to Father Prost; it belongs to him. Now let us say no more."

This brought an abrupt end to the meeting and an end to the controversy. No one could deny the plain truth of Mr. Schneider's words. Shortly after this, in a comparatively peaceful atmosphere, plans were begun

for the new church. The people of the parish were poor,
but they contributed. Some of them, unable to contribute, gave their time and labor to the project.

When Father Neumann came on the scene as pastor, the church was only partially completed and he
faced a debt of $17,000. In order to systematize things,
he started a Church Building Society and asked each parishioner to contribute five cents a week. The people responded cheerfully to this modest appeal. The names of
parishioners appointed by Father Neumann to make
collections were posted in the rear of the temporary
church, so there would be no misunderstanding about
who was authorized to collect. This settled, the new pastor set about familiarizing himself with the various con-
tracts for the building project. It was his job to direct the
work, down to the smallest detail.

Each Saturday he had to meet the payroll for the
men working on the building. On many a Friday night
he lacked money to make up this quota, but he always
managed to raise enough money for the wages of the
workers, before the weekly deadline arrived.

These were trying days for the new pastor who, by
temperament, was not keenly interested in financial
matters and did not feel himself to be adept in this field.
On one occasion a parishioner who had loaned a large
sum of money for the new church heard rumors that St.
Philomena's was in bad shape financially and that his
money was not safe. He rushed to the rectory and asked
Father Neumann for his money. The pastor was alarmed
by this request. He was not in a position to meet this
abrupt demand, yet he knew that if this man told his
friends his request had been refused, others would try to
withdraw their loans, and the financial program of the
parish would be in chaos.

Father Neumann, realizing that a crisis was at
hand, quietly asked the man: "Do you wish the money in

gold or silver?" The man's fears were calmed by this attitude. He felt satisfied that his money was safe and he withdrew his demand.

As the building project continued, Father Neumann managed to surmount each threatening financial crisis, major or minor. And he also was kept busy with general pastoral duties. His parishioners were not all Germans. He had to deal with immigrants from other lands and in this he was aided by his familiarity with several languages. In addition to English and German, he spoke Bohemian, French, Spanish and Italian.

He found time to compile a catechism and to write a Bible History, for use in instructing school children. There were three schools under his direction in the parish, with hundreds of students in attendance. He was keenly interested in education and voiced his opinion on this subject in forthright words.

"The school system of the United States is very liberal in theory," he said, "but in reality it is most intolerant towards Catholics. Every one has to contribute to the erection and maintenance of the public schools, in which instruction is restricted to reading, writing and ciphering. As respects religious instruction, which is excluded from these schools, parents are free to have their children reared in whatever religion they please. Notwithstanding these liberal concessions, it cannot be doubted that the young mind is influenced by the irreligious dispositions of the teacher. Even the textbooks selected for use are injurious to Catholic children. They are nothing less than heretical extracts from a falsified Bible, and histories which contain the most malicious perversion of truth, the grossest lies against the doctrines and practises of the Catholic Church. The teachers are, for the most part, either Protestants or infidels. Immorality reigns in these schools, especially those which are in the country."

He also spoke out against Catholics who sent their children to work in factories when the children should have been in school. And he denounced the custom, prevalent among some Catholics, of entrusting "young children that are a burden to them to respectable and wealthy families by whom they are fed, clothed and instructed until the age of eighteen or twenty." He saw this as a danger to the children's faith and called the custom "a crying evil."

Secret societies were popular in those years and Father Neumann was quick to express his opinion of them. "All assert that the only object of their association is fraternal benevolence and mutual support," he declared. "But this is merely a specious cloak. The very oath tendered them, viz., secrecy as to what goes on in their meetings, is a sufficient reason to suspect their intentions and to warn Catholics against communication with them. The show of philanthropy and the temporal advantages they offer their members have induced the major part of German Protestants to swell their ranks. Under pain of exclusion from the Sacraments, the Provincial Council has forbidden Catholics to join such societies. Notwithstanding the prohibition many have been enticed to join them, and the consequences are that they have fallen away from the faith."

Father Neumann realized that among the German people there was a strong inclination to join societies, including not only secret societies, but others, such as political or literary groups. He catered to this inclination by organizing societies to vitalize the spiritual life of his parishioners. The Confraternity of the Sacred Hearts of Jesus and Mary, the Confraternity for a Good Death and the Confraternity of the Rosary were established in the parish. These groups, with their special meetings and prayers, strengthened the spiritual life of the people and did much to create an atmosphere of solidarity, a vast improvement over the friction of the earlier years.

This was an era in which anti-Catholic feeling was intense in many areas throughout the country. Some people took the position that Catholics were ignorant and superstitious and that they constituted a menace to the American way of life. This conflict between Catholics and anti-Catholics reached the emotional pitch of mob violence in several parts of the country. In Philadelphia St. Augustine's Church was burned down. Father Neumann and his assistants and parishioners were aware of the temper of the times but St. Philomena's escaped harm.

As the day-to-day life at St. Philomena's went on, Father Neumann continued to visit missionary territory in addition to his parish work. These missionary visits, to settlements outside of Pittsburgh, contributed to the eventual establishment of fifteen parishes. As was his custom, Father Neumann continued to drive himself in the matter of doing whatever work was to be done, whether it was visiting missions, instructing converts, or spending long hours in the confessional. He had two very dutiful assistants, but he was the one who made sick calls at night. When one of his assistants suggested that the pastor delegate this duty to him, Father Neumann only smiled and said: "You need all the sleep you can get. I cannot sleep at night, so I might as well go myself."

The assistants were somewhat in the position of the little boy who, for years, thought his mother never slept, since she was awake when he went to sleep and awake when he got up. Father Neumann's pattern of duty was the same; he would be awake and lighting the fire in the morning before the assistants arose, and when day was done and they retired he would still be awake, praying far into the night.

In 1845, on a bright, sunlit day in April, fire swept through Pittsburgh, destroying one third of the city and causing damage estimated as high as $8,000,000. The fire began at about noon in the backyard of an ice house, where a washerwoman had kindled an open fire to heat some water and had left the fire unattended. The flames spread to the ice house and, fanned by a strong wind, swept through twenty city blocks.

Thousands of persons gathered to watch, almost unbelieving, as the fire, like a huge monster, moved through the city, with a wind-driven shower of sparks before it. Firemen battled frantically but futilely to halt the blaze. The spectators fully anticipated that the fire would be checked. When it was not, they ran in terror to save their own homes and possessions. Many tried in vain to summon draymen to move their furniture and other belongings, which they had piled in the street. Looters swooped down, taking what they could before the fire consumed the rest.

After about eight hours, the fire burned itself out. The gas works, several ironworks, a half dozen hotels, the custom house, and hundreds of other buildings had been destroyed. More than 10,000 people were homeless. In spite of the fury of the flames and the wide area of destruction, only two lives were lost. Contributions in money, food and clothing were sent from all parts of the country to aid the fire victims.

At St. Philomena's, which was not in the path of the flames, Father Neumann ordered a special collection for those made destitute by the fire.

CHAPTER SEVEN

While Father Neumann served as pastor at St. Philomena's, important events transpired on the national scene, or loomed ahead in the life of the country.

James Knox Polk was inaugurated President in 1845, after his victory over President Tyler. In his campaign, Polk favored the annexation of land which later became the Oregon Territory. Controversy over this issue spawned the slogan: "Fifty-four forty or fight," a reference to the northern latitude boundary of Oregon and the boundary dispute with Great Britain. Another important factor in the campaign was Polk's stand in favor of the annexation of Texas. Texas was admitted to the Union in 1845, Oregon in 1859. An historical highlight of Polk's administration was the Mexican War, a conflict which grew out of the Texas annexation.

But Father Neumann's own immediate problems crowded from his mind any lengthy preoccupation with the national picture. The project of building the new church was a continuing chore. And the spiritual welfare of his parishioners was constantly in his thoughts. Some religious sects tried in an unusual way to lure Catholics from their faith. Catholic families, living close to poverty and want, were approached with the proposition that if they abandoned their religion they would be given temporal rewards. There would be work at good wages for the unemployed head of the family and there would be money provided at once to ease the pinch of poverty. Some Catholics succumbed to these appeals.

To combat this form of proselytizing, and to ward off other threats to the spiritual welfare of his people, Father Neumann took no dramatic steps. He aided the poor and the jobless whenever he could, an activity in which he was always interested, and, in addition, he set forth a simple, basic program: "Divine service must be conducted with as much solemnity as possible," he said. "Solid and popular sermons and instructions must be preached on Sundays and holy days; confraternities must be introduced; newspapers and good books must be diffused; but, above all, prayer and the frequentation of the sacraments must be insisted upon."

Father Frederick De Held, Provincial of the Belgian Province, under whose authority the Redemptorists in America functioned at that time, made an official visitation to the American houses in 1845. Later, he remarked: "Father Neumann is a great man. He unites eminent prudence and firmness of character with true piety. Were it not that I have already appointed Father Czackert as my vice-regent in America, I would choose Father Neumann for that post."

As the weeks and months went by, the Church of St. Philomena neared completion. In its finished form, it was a beautiful Gothic structure. The people were proud of it and happy to see the culmination of all their efforts and sacrifices. Father Neumann shared their joy, on the first Sunday in October, 1846 — the Feast of the Holy Rosary — when St. Philomena's was dedicated. Bishop O'Connor presided at the dedication ceremonies. The Mayor of Pittsburgh was among those present. The dedication was a victory for Father Neumann in the long struggle to raise sufficient funds for the project. It marked the happy ending of the sometimes frantic efforts to see that the workmen were paid and the building

operation went on without interruption. His feat in ac-
complishing this task was regarded with amazement in
many quarters. Bishop O'Connor remarked at a later
date that Father Neumann had built a church without
money. After the church was dedicated, Father Neumann turned his attention almost at once to the building
of a rectory.

He also continued his tireless pace in performing his
pastoral duties and his usual visits to the outmissions.
With the passage of time, this constant exertion began
to sap his strength. His assistants urged him to relax his
efforts, but their pleas went unheeded. They were worried about his frequent coughing and they became
alarmed when they noticed that he was spitting blood.
To their pleadings he answered: "It is nothing. I shall be
well soon." The assistants felt obliged to notify Father
Czackert, the American Superior, of Father Neumann's
condition and as a result Father Neumann was given a
peremptory order to consult a doctor.

The doctor examined him thoroughly and pre-
scribed immediate rest. Father Czackert, informed of
the doctor's decree, wrote to Father Joseph Mueller, one
of Father Neumann's assistants: "I am very sorry that
your otherwise praiseworthy superior has ruined his
health through his indiscreet zeal. I do not think that I
am doing him any particular injustice when I say so, because even the best and most beautiful virtue loses its
worth if it is exercised without regard to time and circumstances. Without doubt there are still many souls to
be converted in Baltimore, Pittsburgh, etc., but there is
also no doubt that it is not the will of God to lead them
on the way of piety and the fear of God, regardless of
prudence and one's spiritual welfare. Since the in-
disposition, or more correctly, the sickness of Father
Neumann seems to be continuing (when I left him he
was sick) and since his three-year term of office has al-

ready passed, I wish accordingly that Your Reverence inform him that he is to leave Pittsburgh as soon as his health allows.

"I hope he will not take this announcement as an insult, but as a real act of sincere charity. I am only doing what is necessary. Without doubt, if he continues as he is, he may have to face an early death."

Father Neumann left Pittsburgh for Baltimore on January 27, 1847. At the rectory of St. Alphonsus' Church in Baltimore, obedient to the orders of his Superior, he devoted his time to rest and recuperation. He had no way of knowing that, while he rested and recuperated, an important change in his career was imminent.

Near the end of Father Neumann's pastorate in Pittsburgh, Father De Held, in far-off Belgium, surveyed the Redemptorists' work in the United States and he was not happy with what his survey revealed. More than a year had passed since he returned from his visitation to the American houses. At that time, he was firmly convinced that the expansion of the order in America had been too rapid. There were too few priests for the work at hand and he was worried about the debts contracted in America, a total of approximately $100,000. He decided that the order should take on no new foundations or building projects until the Redemptorist ranks were augmented and the debt of the order in the United States reduced. Now, toward the end of 1846, contemplating the way things had gone since he made these decisions, Father De Held was not at all pleased with the current state of affairs.

Father De Held had been put in charge of the American houses in 1844, by Father Passerat, the Vicar General, whose headquarters were in Vienna. Father Passerat had relinquished his American rule to Father De Held when the Austrian government prohibited him from ruling the order in any country outside of Austria.

This arrangement, plus other factors, led to strains and tensions in the administration of the order's activities in America. It was possible for American Redemptorists to appeal directly to Father Passerat, thus bypassing Father De Held. The latter did not always see eye to eye with Father Passerat and this situation generated unrest among some of the Redemptorists in this country.

Father Czackert, as American Superior, bore the responsibility of carrying out Father De Held's orders. But the authority of Father Czackert was limited by some rather strict rules set down by Father De Held. For example, Father Czackert was forbidden to spend more than $100 without Father De Held's express permission. There were also restrictions on making journeys, restrictions which Father Czackert and his subordinates must have found inhibiting and irksome. Most important of the regulations were those prohibiting new foundations and new building projects, without written permission from Father De Held. German and French immigrants were beseeching the American Redemptorists to serve them in various parts of America. The bishops were echoing these pleas, and all of this, together with the fact that Father De Held was many miles away and communication was slow, added to the stresses and strains.

It became clear to Father De Held after his return to Belgium that it was one thing to set up regulations governing the Redemptorists in America, but quite another thing to thus guarantee that everything would go forward as planned. Father De Held himself ran into difficulties when he arrived in Vienna. He learned that some American bishops were urging Father Passerat to establish two more foundations in the United States, in Texas and Oregon. He objected so strongly that the projects were postponed. But the incident illustrates the fact that with authority resting in both Austria and Belgium, and with Father Passerat in Vienna holding final authority over Father De Held, discord among Father De Held's subordinates was a potent menace.

In America after Father De Held's visit, bishops were urging the Redemptorists to start new foundations in New Orleans, Detroit, and Washington, D. C. Father Czackert had visited New Orleans, even before Father De Held's visitation. He made such a favorable impression that the bishop had a church built in New Orleans and was holding it for the Redemptorists. Vienna had approved the foundation, before Father De Held's visit. Now, with Father De Held firmly against expansion, Father Czackert was holding the matter in abeyance.

A Redemptorist was sent to Washington, D. C., to take care of Germans in that area. A weekend mission visit from Baltimore could have sufficed, but this Redemptorist stayed on the scene and within a few months had laid the cornerstone for a church. Father De Held had anticipated no such development.

Similarly, in Detroit, a Redemptorist arrived in response to pleas from the bishop, to serve the Germans in that city. A contract was entered into between the Redemptorists and the bishop. Father De Held knew nothing of this.

To add to his exasperation, Father De Held heard a report that a Redemptorist had gone to New Orleans. "Why have I not been informed of this matter?" Father De Held asked. "I hope that Father Czackert has not started something in that place again."

It developed later that the Redemptorist in New Orleans, Father Louis Gillet, had gone to New Orleans to give a mission and to secure funds for a church at Monroe, Michigan, an established foundation. But the report he had heard about New Orleans served to increase the irritation Father De Held felt on learning of the developments in Washington and Detroit. He decided that something had to be done to keep the Redemptorist houses in America operating in the pattern he had decreed. He arrived at a plan of action and put it into motion by addressing a letter to Father Neumann.

"I have become convinced," he wrote, "that Father Czackert harmonized so little with my views and showed himself so ready to take things into his own hands, as in the case of the missions at Washington and Detroit, that it is impossible for me to retain him any longer as my vice-regent. I have given Father Kannamueller letters for Your Reverence appointing you my temporary vice-regent, and I beg and beseech you to take this office out of love of the Congregation."

When Father Neumann heard this news he had been in Baltimore only about two weeks, after leaving Pittsburgh. The letter was dated December 15, 1846, and Father Neumann received it on February 9, 1847, an arresting example of how slow the transatlantic mail service was in that era.

Father Neumann read Father De Held's letter and he was stunned by it. He had never thought of himself as a vice-regent, even a temporary one. Moreover, he was well aware of the difficulties besetting anyone who took on the duties of the office. He might have preferred to remain simply one of the members of the order, without the anxieties attendant on an executive post. He might have wished to continue to rest after his illness. But, if these thoughts occurred to him, he did not mention them. He accepted the call to duty, just as he had accepted the order to leave St. Philomena's.

Father Neumann was now thirty-five years old. He had been a member of the Congregation of the Most Holy Redeemer for only five years. In his new office, he would have authority over forty priests, many of them older and more experienced than himself. He would direct the operations of about a dozen foundations, including the ones in Washington and Detroit, acceptance of which Father De Held wished him to postpone. In the climate of the Congregation at that time, Father Neumann could expect stormy times, problems and trials. In accepting the office, he accepted all these future hazards. He was now, for the glory of God, and with a much wider field for his harvest of souls, the Superior of the Redemptorists in America.

CHAPTER EIGHT

When he assumed his new office as American Superior, or Vice-regent, Father Neumann had before him a clear-cut directive from Father De Held to accept no new foundations in this country.

"Your Reverence can render the Congregation the greatest service since I know that according to your view no new station will be accepted until the old ones are sufficiently strengthened," Father De Held wrote. "I look upon the contrary system followed so far as the main reason for all the misery in America. I also authorize Your Reverence to reject the foundations in Washington and Detroit, the acceptance of which was not according to rule and consequently was invalid as far as the Congregation is concerned. Delay their acceptance until better times."

Father Neumann was in full agreement with Father De Held that no new foundations should be established. But he was faced with the fact that Redemptorists were already stationed in Washington and Detroit. It would be a matter of months until Father Martin Starck, representing Father De Held, made a visit to America and helped straighten out this and other problems.

Meanwhile, other unpleasant situations crowded in upon the new Superior. Father Simon Sanderl, who had done inspiring work among the Indians as an early Redemptorist in this country, left his station at Monroe,

Michigan, and went to Canada. Father Neumann made earnest pleas that he return, but Father Sanderl did not come back.

This was the climax of difficulties which began for Father Sanderl a few years previously. While stationed in Baltimore, he incurred the disfavor of the archbishop of the area and was transferred to Monroe. He did not go directly to Monroe and Father Czackert, then Superior, ordered him to report to Monroe on a particular date or be dismissed from the Congregation. Later, on learning that Father Sanderl had not arrived as ordered, Father Czackert sent the dismissal paper to Father Louis Gillet, in charge at Monroe. On his arrival, Father Sanderl explained that he had fallen from a horse and broken his leg; he had spent six weeks at a farmhouse. In view of this, Father Gillet didn't mention the dismissal paper.

Later, there came a day when the two priests had a disagreement and a heated argument. Both had fiery temperaments. During the argument, Father Gillet remarked that Father Sanderl should feel gratitude to him, since he had never served the dismissal paper. Father Sanderl, hearing of the dismissal paper for the first time, was crushed. He wondered if he were, in fact, still a member of the order. He left Monroe and went to Canada. He acquired some funds and planned a trip to the Holy Land.

It was at this point that Father Neumann appealed to Father Sanderl to rejoin his confreres. But Father Sanderl did not return. He was subsequently released from his vows and years later he joined the Trappists. He died a holy death as a Trappist at Gethsemane, Kentucky. But this happy ending to the story was not known to Father Neumann when he made fervent pleas to Father Sanderl to return. It added to Father Neumann's woes to think that even one of the sons of St. Alphonsus was wandering the world outside the Congregation.

Father Gillet also became involved in difficulties. In an effort to raise funds for the Monroe foundation, he visited New Orleans. This was contrary to Father De Held's ban on traveling. He had previously incurred the displeasure of Father De Held and the latter had told Father Neumann that Father Gillet could not remain long at Monroe as Superior. Father Neumann recalled Father Gillet, the latter's three years as Superior having expired, and this action proved to be a heavy blow to Father Gillet.

Father Kannamueller, lately arrived from Europe, spoke to Father Gillet in such a way that Father Gillet's temper was aroused and he wrote to Father De Held, asking a dispensation from his vows. Father De Held refused the request, apparently hoping, as Father Neumann hoped, that Father Gillet would change his mind. But, assigned to a German parish in New York, Father Gillet was disturbed by the fact that his eloquent French was of no use. He continued to seek a dispensation and Father Neumann continued to delay the action. As a matter of fact, Father Neumann's powers were quite limited. He himself had no power to grant a dispensation. Father Gillet eventually was dispensed from his vows. He spent several years in dioceses in the eastern part of the United States and also visited South America. Later, in France, he joined the Celestine branch of the Cistercian Order. Like Father Sanderl, his life was crowned by a holy death many years later. But, as in the case of Father Sanderl, his ultimate fate was unknown to Father Neumann as the latter tried in vain to persuade him to remain in the Congregation.

These cases weighed heavily on Father Neumann's mind as he administered the Redemptorist foundations and the outlying mission stations.

One of the foundations under Father Neumann's care was a colony known as St. Mary's, in Pennsylvania.

This was a tract of 35,000 acres in Elk County, in the northwestern part of the state. It was tenanted by about 2,000 settlers. About five years before Father Neumann became the American Superior, St. Mary's was founded by German families of Baltimore and Philadelphia. The original intent was to establish a German Catholic community. The motivation was largely an effort to escape anti-Catholic sentiment. Father Sanderl visited the colony in the spring of 1843 and enabled many in the colony to make their Easter duty. Father Alexander, the Superior, became interested in the project as a Redemptorist foundation and invested $10,000 in its future. A church and a school were built there.

But it soon became evident that the land was not very productive. This, coupled with the fact that the colony was far removed from any populous center made it apparent that maintenance of the colony would be a problem. King Ludwig of Bavaria was among those who contributed to maintaining the colony. Father Alexander kept the Redemptorists there, hoping that conditions would improve. Father De Held, while not enthusiastic about St. Mary's, was satisfied to let it remain a Redemptorist foundation.

The colony of St. Mary's never did prosper through these years, and eventually it was turned over to the Benedictines. But, in a rather indirect way, the colony had an important bearing on Father Neumann's work in the parish of St. Alphonsus in Baltimore.

In the summer of 1847 five of the School Sisters of Notre Dame arrived in America from Munich, to help the colony of St. Mary's. Mother Theresa, the Superior, hoped to establish at St. Mary's the motherhouse of the order in this country. The nuns hoped to teach at St. Mary's and at other schools throughout the United States. Mother Theresa was greatly disturbed when she was advised by people she talked with in this country that St. Mary's would not be at all suitable as a mother-house. It was pointed out that St. Mary's was too isolated and was not in a sound financial condition.

Mother Theresa went to Baltimore to get Father Neumann's opinion. He agreed that St. Mary's was not a wise choice. However, having come this far, Mother Theresa and her companions decided to make the trip to St. Mary's and look over the site. It was a long, tiresome and tragic journey. One of the nuns died when they reached Harrisburg. Later, when Mother Theresa and her little band visited St. Mary's and saw the huddle of shabby houses in the woods they felt their whole trip from Munich had been a mistake.

Father Starck, touring the American foundations, happened to be at St. Mary's when the nuns arrived. They were made welcome, but Father Starck was distressed to learn that they did not have an invitation from Bishop O'Connor of Pittsburgh to come to the diocese. He suggested that Mother Theresa visit Bishop O'Connor. This she did, leaving the other nuns at St. Mary's and going to Pittsburgh. Bishop O'Connor was not pleased at their arrival without his invitation, but he was agreeable to their staying at St. Mary's.

By this time, however, Mother Theresa knew that St. Mary's would never do as a motherhouse and she returned to Baltimore, still in quest of a headquarters for her order in America. Father Neumann made the suggestion that the School Sisters of Notre Dame teach in his parish of St. Alphonsus. Mother Theresa agreed and Father Neumann sold the order a building which was formerly a Redemptorist novitiate. It was the beginning of years of fruitful association in the field of education between the Redemptorists and the School Sisters of Notre Dame. One of these pioneer nuns was Mother Caroline, later Superior of the School Sisters of Notre Dame.

Father Starck finished his American visitation in the fall of 1847 and departed for Europe. Before he left, he officially confirmed the appointment of Father Neumann, but the appointment continued to be a temporary one, awaiting the final approval of Father Passerat in Vienna. Father Neumann's executive powers were not increased in any way; he was still under the rules laid down by Father De Held. But Father Starck did officially approve the New Orleans foundation and the Detroit foundation. The foundation at Washington was not approved. These decisions helped to clarify Father Neumann's responsibilities.

Father Czackert went happily down to New Orleans to take charge of the foundation there. He thus fulfilled not only his own dream of a Redemptorist foundation in New Orleans, but the dream of many members of the order. This dream dated to the times of St. Alphonsus and was a part of the Redemptorist lore. The story was told that St. Alphonsus was walking with a group of students along the shore of the Bay of Naples. He noticed a ship on which were the words: "For New Orleans." Calling the attention of his students to the words, St. Alphonsus said: "My sons will one day have a house in that place."

Before he left for Europe, Father Starck appointed two consultors to Father Neumann. One was Father Alexander, who had formerly served as American Superior. The other was Father Ignatius Stelzig, who had made the trip to America with Father Starck. Father Stelzig was an earnest and brilliant young priest. He was only twenty-four years of age and had been ordained only about a year. He had fine literary talent; during his lifetime he wrote fourteen books.

There were times when his writing, in letters to Father Starck, was critical of Father Neumann. Father Stelzig wrote of the sale of the building to the School

Sisters of Notre Dame, saying in effect that the sale at
the original cost, rather than the higher market price at
the time of the sale, indicated that Father Neumann did
not have the order's financial interests at heart. Father
Stelzig apparently did not put the same value Father
Neumann put on the good will of the nuns and their importance in establishing a solid foundation of religious
education in the parish.

On another occasion, Father Stelzig wrote: "Father
Neumann has only half the necessary qualities of a good
Superior, namely, exemplary conduct and regularity. He
lacks the all important quality in America of force or authority. He never had this and he never will."

This appraisal was no doubt influenced by Father
Neumann's small stature and his habitual quiet and
gentle manner. He was described by one of his confreres
as "so quiet and so docile." A parishioner in Baltimore
remarked: "No one could tell from his manner of acting
that he was a Superior."

On one occasion, visiting a Redemptorist foundation in New York, his appearance was so unimpressive
that the porter at the rectory thought he was a sacristan,
performing some routine errand. When Father Neumann asked to see the pastor, the porter asked him to sit
on a bench and wait. When the pastor appeared and
knelt before Father Neumann for his blessing, the porter
was overcome with embarrassment in not recognizing
the Superior. But Father Neumann spoke kindly to the
young man and was amused by the incident.

Father De Held, in informing one of the Redemptorists of the appointment of Father Neumann, had referred to him as "the wisest, the greatest and the best
among all the Redemptorists in America."

Apparently undisturbed by either praise or blame,
if indeed he was aware of it, Father Neumann pursued
his quiet way. He discovered that a young lady who had

been teaching in the parochial school had two years' back pay coming to her. She did not ask for it, but Father Neumann insisted that she take it.

His attitude toward parochial duties is revealed in a letter to his parents. It is characteristic of him that he made no mention of his new office as Superior.

"The reason of my long silence is that nothing new has occurred either to brother Wenceslaus or myself," he wrote. "The former is now in Pittsburgh and I am in Baltimore. Our German parish is always on the increase. Before I went to Pittsburgh, two priests could more easily accomplish here what it now requires seven to perform. We have charge of three schools, and Protestants are constantly coming for instruction in our holy religion. They generally end by entering the Church, after which many of them show their gratitude to God by leading a Christian life such as is seldom witnessed in Europe. Eighty-five adults, one third of them Negroes, were last year received into the Church."

A phase of his work which seemed to appeal particularly to Father Neumann was the activity of the mission stations. In addition to the foundations, there were seventy mission stations under his jurisdiction. He not only supervised the work of these stations, but he visited the stations himself. This was the kind of apostolic labor he was familiar with. He was at home in the log cabin chapels, and on the long jaunts to and from the stations.

He was also eager to have the Redemptorists give missions at parishes around the country, in response to frequent requests for their services. In this field, too, he played an active part, joining his confreres in the mission work, sharing in the preaching and spending hours in the confessional.

He also followed closely the growth of the parochial schools in his Baltimore parish. He enjoyed visiting the classrooms and sometimes took over the instruction himself. He had a special talent for teaching children, particularly catechism, and his gentle spirit seemed to find a kinship with the youngsters.

Mother Caroline of the School Sisters of Notre Dame wrote of Father Neumann as a teacher: "His glance seemed to have something in it of the all-seeing attribute of God, so did it penetrate souls. The children often said to me: 'Sister, Father Neumann looked right into my heart.'

"I had a habit of speaking in a high voice and losing my patience while teaching," Mother Caroline wrote, "but after Father Neumann surprised me in this fault once or twice, I learned to correct it. He used to enter the schoolroom so modestly and so quietly that I did not notice him until he greeted me with the words: 'Sister, I thought I heard you screaming just now,' and then he would fix his large expressive eyes on me so earnestly that there was no mistaking the meaning."

A troublesome lad was causing the teachers, and his father, grave concern. The teachers wanted the student dismissed. Father Neumann interested himself in the case and tutored the boy for a time, spending an hour a day with him. Under Father Neumann's influence the boy's improvement in his attitude and deportment astounded his father and the nuns.

All such activity on Father Neumann's part reflected his keen interest in the parochial schools and the importance he placed on them in the spiritual life of the people. It reflected also his keen interest in each individual under his care.

It was a segment of the many chores, large and small, which he regarded as vital in gathering his harvest of souls.

CHAPTER NINE

On Baltimore's North Park Street was a convent which housed members of the Oblate Sisters of Providence, an order of colored nuns who had accomplished much good for the colored children of the area. Shortly after Father Neumann assumed his duties as vice-regent he learned that these colored nuns might have to disband.

Archbishop Samuel Eccleston of Baltimore, under whose authority the nuns functioned, felt that it was best that the order be dissolved. In his opinion, the nuns had shown some good results, but their venture, overall, had been a failure. Their numbers had dwindled; they lacked funds and needed spiritual assistance. The archbishop thought the best solution to the problem was for the few remaining nuns to disband and seek work as servants in the Baltimore area.

When Father Neumann heard of the plight of the order, he sent a Redemptorist, Father Thaddeus Anwander, to talk with the archbishop on behalf of the nuns. Father Neumann picked a good man. Father Anwander, when he was at first told by the archbishop that there was no point in postponing the disbanding of the order, fell on his knees and pleaded that the order be allowed to continue. The archbishop, impressed by Father Anwander's fervor, gave his permission for the order to continue.

Father Neumann then interested himself actively in the welfare of these colored nuns. The membership, reduced to three, quickly rose to sixteen. Their pupils, only fifteen in number, were soon increased to more than 100. Father Neumann became the confessor of the order and gave the members instruction in the spiritual life. Mass was said in the convent chapel twice a week. Every Sunday Father Neumann gave Benediction in the chapel and he was always eager to aid the nuns in any project. Today, members of the Oblate Sisters of Providence remember with prayerful gratitude Father Neumann's interest in their welfare and Father Anwander's zealous concern at this crucial period in their history.

On the higher executive level of administering the Redemptorist affairs throughout the country, Father Neumann did not find a comparable satisfaction. He seemed to be constantly moving through a maze of difficulties which seldom could be solved by quick and decisive action.

From the beginning of his term as vice-regent he was beset by pleas to begin new foundations or to enlarge existing foundations, action which would run counter to the wishes of his Superior, Father De Held. A simple refusal did not always settle the matter. One of his more zealous confreres would begin a new development and then advise Father Neumann of his action and ask approval. In another case, a pastor whould claim tacit approval of extension plans by Vienna authorities, superior to Father De Held. Since communication with Europe was a long process, plans for a new church could be under way before word was received negating the venture. At this point, stopping the work was not always a practical move.

Meanwhile, the debt of the Redemptorists in America was more than $150,000 and reaching toward $200,000. This was not an alarming figure, compared with debts of other missionary orders during that period. But the Redemptorists were dealing mostly with poor immigrants who had difficulty in supporting themselves, much less contributing to church support. Records disclose that the first time services were held in St. Peter's Church in Philadelphia the collection amounted to only $1.40.

Among those requesting the Redemptorists' help during Father Neumann's term as vice-regent was the Right Reverend Francis Patrick Kenrick, Bishop of Philadelphia. The Redemptorists already were in charge of St. Peter's parish in Philadelphia and Bishop Kenrick was pleased with their work. But Father Neumann, adhering to the policy against expansion, declined Bishop Kenrick's second request.

It is interesting to note that the lives of Bishop Kenrick and Father Neumann touched at this point. Once before, when Father Neumann was a young, unordained priest in his native land, seeking a call to an American diocese, Father Herman Dichtl, a canon of Budweis Cathedral, had thought of sending him to the Philadelphia Diocese, in response to an appeal from Bishop Kenrick. The latter had asked Canon Andreas Rass, director of a seminary in Strasbourg, to send two German priests. For a time Father Neumann had looked forward hopefully to being given an assignment in the Philadelphia Diocese, but even before he sailed from Europe he knew that this was not to be. He heard from Father John Martin Henni, a missionary priest lately returned from America, that there was no longer a need for a German priest in Philadelphia. Canon Rass subsequently confirmed this, telling Father Neumann that he was not needed in Philadelphia. This was one of the incidents in the pattern of frustration that Father Neumann faced before he sailed for America.

Later in his life, Father Neumann was to find in

Bishop Kenrick a staunch admirer and a true friend, through a period of tension and severe trial.

Struggling with his problems as vice-regent, Father Neumann found, at the end of his first year, that no serious calamity had overtaken the affairs of the order. True, things were far from ideal, but the parishes throughout the country had kept expenses within income, with two exceptions, Rochester and Philadelphia. These centers had been unable to pay the interest on their debts. Rochester in particular was a problem. Father Neumann made a hurried trip to that city and was able to avert foreclosure on church property. In Detroit, the problems of trusteeism created a serious situation. The lay trustees would not allow the Redemptorists the freedom they wished to have, to run the church and parish affairs as they thought best. The matter eventually was settled in court, where the Redemptorists won. As one commentator remarked, some trustees of this period would have liked to dictate the number of candles that should be lighted on the altar. By suffering through unpleasantness created by the trustees, Father Neumann and his confreres played heroic roles and did much to eliminate the evils of trusteeism for future pastors.

On the spiritual side, the order was flourishing. Father Neumann stressed self-sanctification as the goal the sons of St. Alphonsus should constantly strive for and he required a strict observance of the rule of the order from all in his charge. New aspirants to the priesthood were enrolled in the seminary, to become future Redemptorists. St. Peter's Church in Philadelphia was consecrated, the first Redemptorist church to be consecrated in this country.

In New York City, where there had been some troublesome misunderstandings about whether or not permission to build had been granted, St. Alphonsus' Church was dedicated. Also in New York, worshippers crowded into the little frame Church of the Most Holy Redeemer. The sons of St. Alphonsus sought out other avenues for bringing spiritual comfort to troubled souls, by visiting the almshouses and asylums on Ward's Island, Blackwell's Island and Randall's Island in the New York area.

From Monroe, Michigan, came encouraging reports of the growth of the Sisters of the Immaculate Heart of Mary, an order founded by Father Louis Gillet. As related previously, Father Gillet subsequently got into difficulties and was dispensed from his vows, but died a holy death as a Cistercian. Today, the Sisters of the Immaculate Heart of Mary occupy an important niche in parochial school work in this country, a beautiful flowering of the seed planted years ago by Father Gillet.

One tour of duty by Father Neumann stands out as a milestone in its accomplishments for the benefit of the Redemptorist parishes and in the matter of accenting Redemptorist interest in developing parochial schools. Father Neumann, with Mother Caroline, now Superior of the School Sisters of Notre Dame, and another nun of the order, traveled to Milwaukee and then to Detroit and Buffalo, completing their journey with a trip down the Atlantic seaboard to Baltimore. They visited the Redemptorist parishes and, as a result, the School Sisters of Notre Dame agreed to take charge of schools in Pittsburgh, Buffalo and Philadelphia. They also agreed to staff the school of the Most Holy Redeemer in New York at a future date.

Some time afterwards, Mother Caroline recalled incidents of the 2,000-mile journey. At one point, a stranger cursed Father Neumann, but Father Neumann ignored the man. At another time, some mischievous boys marked Father Neumann's coat with chalk while he was taking a nap on the deck of a boat. On awakening, when the nuns noticed the chalk marks, Father Neumann calmly brushed them away, remarking: "It will soon wash off." Under insult, he always ignored the affront and continued to go quietly about his business.

Mother Caroline ended her recollection with a heart-felt tribute to Father Neumann. No doubt, as she wrote, her thoughts went back to the arrival of herself and other nuns, in the little band who came to America from Munich, and visited the bleak colony at St. Mary's in Pennsylvania, their future unknown and, at that moment, unpromising.

"This man of God," Mother Caroline wrote, "was in truth the instrument of Divine Providence in spreading and firmly establishing the Congregation of the School Sisters in the United States. . . . We were so happy to have him for our confessor and spiritual adviser. We had ample time and opportunity for discovering his learning, his kindheartedness, and his sanctity. . . . Between the years 1847 and '52 he must have trodden the road from St. Alphonsus' to St. James' at least a thousand times to hear our confessions and to give us conferences, retreats, etc. . . . His zeal for souls was simply indefatigable. He showed the deepest interest in our ceremonies, particularly those of reception to the habit and the profession of vows. We were extremely happy under his wise and paternal direction. We have indeed every reason to revere him as our founder in America."

Father Neumann was able to make this admirable impression on nuns under his direction, but he was not able to make a similar impression on all of his confreres, nor on his Superiors abroad. It seems ironic that, while all revered him as a man of piety and character, some found fault with him as an administrator.

The difficulties no doubt had their roots in the fact that Father Neumann was vice-regent only on a temporary basis, and this tended to weaken his authority with those in his charge. There was also the fact that his authority was limited, circumscribed by the regulations laid down by Father De Held in Belgium. The appointment was temporary because the Redemptorist Superiors in Europe were considering making the American branch of the order a separate Province, since it was difficult to govern from such a distance and also because of conflicts between authorities in Belgium and Austria.

Father De Held, with the intention of clarifying the situation, appealed to authorities in Vienna and in Rome, to have the American houses made a separate Province. Pending this decision, the American houses were placed under the Austrian Province.

Father Neumann found this new development disturbing. He had been striving to carry out his work as ordered by Father De Held. Now, he was faced with the prospect of working under different Superiors, who might interpret his duties differently. At about this time, Father Neumann wrote to his Superiors abroad, telling them some of his problems. He felt that he did not have sufficient authority. He also felt that other problems were due to his own inadequacies. And he said he was thinking of resigning.

Shortly after this, Father Passerat wrote, giving Father Neumann broader powers, "authority to decide every important question in cases that are urgent and unforeseen." Father Passerat also wrote a letter to all the Redemptorists in America, urging them to give Father Neumann full obedience and adding: "Particularly let no one urge that permission be given him to erect any buildings. Rather, let everyone aim and strive to reduce our enormous debts, which, unless God helps us, will ruin several of our missions."

In this letter Father Passerat struck an ominous note. Because of the rising tide of political unrest in Europe, he feared for the future of the sons of St. Alphonsus. He feared that the order, in a wave of an-

ticlerical feeling, might be driven from its European
centers and might have to take refuge in the United
States. Within a year, the things he feared were to
plague the order and the consequences were to have, indirectly, an important effect on Father Neumann's career.

Father Martin Starck, the Austrian Provincial and
now Father Neumann's Superior, wrote to offer Father
Neumann support and understanding. "I expected more
manifestations of dissatisfaction than is evident from
the contents of your letter. It would be asking too much
to expect that no protests arise from any quarter. . . . Let
us thank God that matters are not worse than they are."

Father Passerat also wrote words of encouragement:
"Courage, Reverend and very dear Father, it is obedience, or rather Jesus Christ who has laid the burden of
authority on your shoulders; it is Jesus Christ, then, who
must help you and He will do so. Do not be discouraged
when things do not succeed and the brethren do not obey
you."

In a subsequent letter Father Starck wrote: "Do not
think that you have been forgotten or that support from
here will be wanting. Turn to me in every necessary case
and be assured that I will interest myself in your affairs
and in every circumstance I will obtain help and support. I know the needs of the Congregation in America,
at least in great part, and it will be very pleasing to me
to help you as much as I am able. But do not hope to
have everything go according to your wishes all at once,
or expect to be without contradictions. There is no such
thing in your office and you will not live to see it."

Though vexed by many pressures, Father Neumann
took the time, on February 10, 1848, to become a natu-
ralized citizen of the United States in Baltimore.

Father Neumann continued to wrestle with the
problems of his office, but criticism was being voiced by

some of his confreres. One felt he was giving the order in America weak leadership, while another looked to him in vain for "personal, fear-inspiring authority." One of the Redemptorist Fathers, recalled to Vienna, was said to have brought with him a series of letters, signed by Redemptorists in this country, voicing complaints against Father Neumann and urging that he be recalled from the office of vice-regent. There is reason to believe that this report was true.

In March of 1848, the political unrest which Father Passerat had cited in his letters came to a bloody climax. In Switzerland, France, Bavaria and Austria mobs marched against the reigning governments. In the turmoil that ensued in Austria, Father Passerat found himself exiled to Belgium.

While in Belgium, Father Passerat received permission from Rome to make the Redemptorist houses in America, not a Province, but a Vice-Province. He thereupon informed Father Neumann that he was making him Vice-Provincial of the American houses. "I will relieve you of this burden as soon as I am able, if you so wish," he wrote, "but, dear Father, those who fear an office are most worthy to bear it. There can be no greater consolation for you than the fact that God Himself has placed this burden on you through obedience."

On the face of it, this would seem to make Father Neumann the Vice-Provincial, but the matter was more complex than that. In naming Father Neumann to this office, Father Passerat was required to act with the advice of his consultors, but, being exiled in Belgium, he was without his consultors. He intended to send the formal document of appointment later.

This set of circumstances, routine as they may appear to be, had immediate repercussions. Other officials of the order questioned the legality of Father Neumann's appointment and he himself was thrown into a state of

perplexity. Father Michael Heilig, the new Provincial of
the Belgium Province, wrote to Father Neumann, stating that he wanted to make the appointment in true
canonical form and asking Father Neumann, in effect, if
he wished the appointment or not. In the meantime, Father Neumann had written to Father Heilig, asking to be
allowed to resign.

And so, on October 7, 1848, Father Heilig wrote to
Father Neumann, announcing the decision to "relieve
him of the burden" of the Vice-Provincialate, and ex-
pressing the thanks of the order for all that he had accomplished as vice-regent. Father Bernard Hafkenscheid was named Vice-Provincial of the Redemptorists
in America.

Father Neumann had ruled the Redemptorists in
America for almost two years. He had effected definite
gains. And he had halted the tendency toward overex-
pansion. As to his own reactions on ending his term as
vice-regent, this is probably best expressed in his own
words.

When reports reached America that letters of com-
plaint had been brought to the Superiors of the order in
Europe, some of Father Neumann's confreres urged him
to reply to these attacks, but Father Neumann simply
smiled and said: "Let it go. Do not be sorry for me. I
have never done anything to become a Superior and I
will not do anything to remain one. On the contrary, I
will thank God if I am relieved of this responsibility."

CHAPTER TEN

Early in 1849 Father Hafkenscheid took over the duties of Vice-Provincial and for Father Neumann there followed a few years of comparative calm. His life was calm, as compared to the hectic experience of being a Superior, and compared to the trying years still in store for him. But his life was still a busy one. He always remembered his earlier resolve, never to waste a minute. And he always remembered to work, directly or indirectly, at his harvest of souls.

One of Father Hafkenscheid's first official acts as Vice-Provincial was to make Father Neumann one of his consultors, or advisers. This gave Father Neumann important responsibilities, but the pressure was less than when he himself was the head. It also served to indicate the confidence Father Hafkenscheid had in him. Father Hafkenscheid referred to Father Neumann as "my right arm," and when the Vice-Provincial had to make a trip to Europe in 1850 he left Father Neumann in charge.

Affairs of the order in America moved at a quieter pace now than when Father Neumann was Vice-Provincial, a condition due in a good measure to Father Neumann's tireless work when he held the office. And so Father Neumann found time for an activity he had always been anxious to engage in. He turned to writing.

In his earlier years writing had been one of his prime interests, but when his priestly duties crowded out such activity he abandoned his writing plans, no doubt waiting for a time when he could again put pen to paper. Father Neumann's interest as a writer centered naturally on catechism, Bible history and theology.

Some years before, in Pittsburgh, he had compiled two catechisms in German and they had wide circulation. Now, in Baltimore, he brought out a new edition of one of these and also worked on a Bible history. Years before he had worked on a Bible history in German and had it published. Now he brought out a second edition of this work and labored on an enlarged version, but this latter book did not reach publication.

The field of theology seemed to absorb him more than any other subject. By his own reading through the years, as well as his basic seminary instruction, he became familiar with the teachings of St. Thomas Aquinas, St. Augustine, St. Alphonsus Liguori and others. He wrote more than 2,000 pages of carefully prepared notes on the writings of these authorities. Doubtless he planned eventual publication of his own writing in this field, but this was not to be. While he worked diligently on his manuscript, he suddenly had to abandon it.

He was named rector of St. Alphonsus Church in Baltimore in January of 1851. Two months later, Father Hafkenscheid returned from abroad and relieved him of his duties as Acting Provincial. Nevertheless, the work as rector of St. Alphonsus Church ruled out any further expenditure of time on writing. Persons familiar with his plans and preparations for his work on theology have voiced regret that he never had the opportunity to complete it.

At St. Alphonsus Church Father Neumann entered zealously into the busy life of a rector in a busy parish. He settled down to what some might consider a dull routine. There were eight priests at St. Alphonsus, an indication of the scope of the parish. And, in addition, Father Neumann presided over St. James' and St. Michael's parishes, which were known as outmissions.

It would be pleasant to record at this point some pious anecdote, some unauthenticated miracle perhaps, which would set Father Neumann's life above the sphere occupied by an ordinary rector. But there were no such happenings. He said Mass and he heard confessions. He preached and he supervised the repair of church property. He baptized people. He performed marriage ceremonies. He administered the last rites to the dying. He visited the outmissions, where this work was repeated.

He was dedicated and hard-working, somewhat like a farmer in his native Bohemia, spending his strength and his energy in sowing seeds and gathering his harvest.

He met with disappointments, the same as other men who lived one-purpose lives leading to other goals. But, through it all, he was persevering, with a patience and courage born of staunch faith. Again, like a Bohemian farmer, he did not falter in the face of storms or droughts or any misfortune, but continued on toward the fruition of his crop and the harvest.

Perhaps the best way to summarize Father Neumann's devotion to duty would be to say that he exemplified the virtues which mark the Redemptorists: humility, simplicity, zeal.

As part of his duties, he was confessor for Francis Patrick Kenrick, now Archbishop of Baltimore. This assignment was a compliment to Father Neumann's spiritual qualities; obviously the archbishop held him in high esteem. This esteem was demonstrated, forcefully and somewhat shockingly to Father Neumann late in the year 1851, when the archbishop suggested that Father Neumann might soon have use for a bishop's mitre.

The idea astounded Father Neumann. He knew

that Archbishop Kenrick had recently been elevated to the Archbishopric of Baltimore after serving twenty years as Bishop of Philadelphia. He knew that a bishop was to be named to replace Kenrick in Philadelphia. But he had never envisioned himself as being chosen for that important see.

Far from being elated over the possibility, Father Neumann appeared to be plunged into gloom. His reaction was swift and definite. He asked the nuns of his parish to make a novena for his intention, and he described this intention as wishing to avoid "a grave calamity to the Church in America."

He then asked Father Hafkenscheid to write to Rome, urging the Redemptorists in that city to try to prevent his being nominated. Father Hafkenscheid did write and the Redemptorists did make a strong appeal to the authorities. They suggested that Father Neumann did not want the bishopric and that he was unsuited for it because of his life as a religious. They said that his vow of poverty would not allow him to accept and that he was needed by the order. The appeal was presented to the Pope, together with the vote of the cardinals in the Sacred Congregation of Propaganda Fide, most of whom favored Father Neumann's appointment. In the final analysis, the decision rested with the Pope.

Meanwhile, the topic of Father Neumann's possible appointment was widely discussed by both clergy and laymen in this country. Father Neumann's confreres, and many of the laity who knew him, were quick to say that Father Neumann was a man of piety, "a holy, zealous and learned man," and to give him similar accolades. But, in many cases, there was an undercurrent of criticism, no doubt sincere, which established a conflict in regard to Father Neumann's qualifications for the bishopric, a conflict which was to be with him as long as he lived.

The gist of the criticism against Father Neumann's appointment was that he was not a polished and imposing figure, did not make a good impression, did not speak English well and was not a good orator. In other words, he was not the type, some felt, to serve as bishop for the sophisticated, urbane segment of his Philadelphia charges.

On the other hand, many were in favor of his appointment because he could speak German and because he knew, understood, and could very well serve the poor, the underprivileged and the lowly in the City of Brotherly Love.

The desire to have a German-speaking bishop in Philadelphia was one which German Catholics felt strongly. There were many of them in Philadelphia and in the outlying parts of the far-flung diocese. German Catholics throughout the United States at that time felt that they should have German-speaking priests, rather than the Irish-Americans who so often served them.

The conflict over Father Neumann's appointment continued for weeks. Archbishop Kenrick placed his name second on the list of three choices which he sent to Rome. The archbishop had placed Father Neumann's name first, but had been persuaded by a fellow-bishop to give first place to Father Edward Purcell, a man highly regarded by many of the bishops. The third name on Archbishop Kenrick's list was that of Father William Elder, who was serving on the faculty of Mount St. Mary's Seminary and College in Maryland.

In a private letter to Father Bernard Smith, rector of the Irish College in Rome, Archbishop Kenrick praised Father Neumann's virtues and said he was the most suitable for the bishopric. Archbishop Kenrick also wrote that it was his personal opinion that Father Neumann's name should be first on the list. This letter later was submitted to the Prefect of Propaganda, James Cardinal Franzoni. In a letter to the Prefect of Propaganda Archbishop Kenrick wrote: "Of the three priests I have commended, Father John Neumann is certainly the most worthy as regards piety, learning, skill in performing ecclesiastical duties and other great qualifications. He speaks both German and English fluently, but I cannot deny that one thing against him in so great a city is the fact that he is a Bohemian and, because of this, not so eloquent and less likely to please the ear. His manners, likewise, are different from those existing in our country."

Archbishop Kenrick urged the archbishops and bishops to write to Rome and give their opinions on the nominations and this they did.

The Bishop of Pittsburgh stated that he thought Father Neumann would make a good bishop. He had previously expressed this opinion to Archbishop Kenrick, though not in relation to the Philadelphia See. Now he stated that he thought Father Neumann would make a good bishop, but, he added: "I would hesitate to commend him for the See of Philadelphia, for although he speaks English well, he cannot preach with distinction and this is absolutely necessary for a bishop."

Another bishop, giving his opinion to Archbishop Kenrick, stated: "The being an Irishman, a native American or an eloquent man (good preacher) are minor qualifications for a bishop. Learning, especially ecclesiastic piety, a good judgment, method or order in business and duties, energy and industry, zeal with prudence, are the higher qualifications. Therefore, I give my name strongly for Father Newman [*sic*]."

The Bishop of Chicago said: "To me, Father Neumann appears the most worthy and the most qualified because in the opinion of everyone he is endowed with all the virtues and abilities to fill such an office."

From the Bishop of Richmond came these words:

"Of those commended in the second and third places, I know very little of their merits and particular qualifications, but in my judgment it is not expedient to choose either of them for this dignity in a city so great, turbulent, difficult and with malignant adversaries of our religion. He who is placed second on the list, Father Neumann, does not speak English well and I fear his election, though favorable to the German-speaking populace, would find very little favor with the American people; and in our country English is the principal language and more necessary for a bishop. . . . As far as I am concerned, Father Purcell is by far the best choice."

Now, with a variety of opinions registered, there remained only the decision of Pope Pius IX.

As far as Father John Neumann's opinion was concerned, he could accurately be placed among the group who did not want Father John Neumann appointed Bishop of Philadelphia. As his personal choice, if he considered his activities from a human point of view without reference to the Divine Will, he would probably prefer to go on quietly with his writing. Or, as an alternative, he no doubt would have been reasonably happy as rector of St. Alphonsus', in spite of, and perhaps because of, the fact that it required all of his energies.

But the thought of being Bishop of Philadelphia, presiding over one of the largest and most important dioceses in the country, must have filled him with a feeling almost akin to terror. After all, he himself had said he was "a strong Bohemian mountain boy," implying that he could accomplish whatever physical feats were necessary on the long mission rounds, in all kinds of weather. But he had never said that he had the suavity, the impressive physical stature, or the oratorical gifts which distinguished Archbishop Kenrick and some of the other leaders of the Catholic Church in America.

His inner feelings must have churned in a turmoil as

he contemplated his possible future as a bishop. And this inner turmoil must have been made more acute because, in his heart, he yearned above everything to do the will of God, regardless of his personal feelings. In his diary we find the lines: "Speak to me, O my God, let me know Thy will, for behold I am ready to fulfill Thy every command. The difficult, the irksome, I will patiently endure for love of Thee." And yet, humanly speaking, it was natural for him to recoil from a task which he foresaw, and accurately foresaw, as one which would bring him heartache, frustration and acute misery.

Official news of the Pope's decision reached Archbishop Kenrick on March 1, 1852. Father John Neumann was appointed as the new Bishop of Philadelphia.

Archbishop Kenrick was delighted with the choice. After receiving the news, the archbishop decided that he would notify Father Neumann personally. He selected a bright, sunny day and strolled from his residence to the St. Alphonsus rectory. Arriving at the rectory, the archbishop went directly to Father Neumann's room, but Father Neumann was out. The archbishop remained a few moments and then left.

When Father Neumann returned and went to his room, he saw two objects on the table which gave him a feeling of intense agitation. Hurriedly summoning the porter, he asked if he had had any visitors. When told that Archbishop Kenrick had been there Father Neumann looked again at the two objects and his agitation increased. The archbishop had left on Father Neumann's table his own episcopal ring and pectoral cross.

The message was clear. Sensing its full import, Father Neumann sank to his knees in prayer. The next morning, when one of the priests of the household looked into the room, Father Neumann was still kneeling in prayer and meditation, unaware that a new day was dawning.

As he arose, doubtless he carried in his heart the prayer which he later adopted as his episcopal motto: "Passion of Christ, strengthen me!"

CHAPTER ELEVEN

Authorities in Rome decreed that the consecration of Father Neumann be held soon, so that he could be present as Bishop of Philadelphia at the First Plenary Council in Baltimore in May. This was a conference of all the bishops in this country. Previously, when the Catholic Church had only one Province in the country, the bishops had met in Council. Now, they were assembling from the Church's several Provinces and, obviously, it was a meeting of prime importance. So the date of Sunday, March 28, 1852 was set for Father Neumann's consecration. It was his forty-first birthday.

Meanwhile, his appointment to the rank of bishop evoked further comment for and against his selection.

"I don't know how to explain this decision," the Bishop of Pittsburgh wrote to a fellow clergyman, "except that in their anxiety to impose some German blood into the episcopal body they laid hold of the first German name that presented itself. . . . I fear that I have much to answer for in bringing his name forward. I mentioned his name to Abp. Kenrick as a person well-suited for the Episcopacy, but I thought of him and spoke of recommending him only in connection with the See of Erie which I then consulted the Abp. about. In my letter to Rome I gave it as my decided opinion that his address or rather want of power in addressing an English audience form, in my opinion, an (insuperable?) objection to his appointment for Philadelphia. I suppose God has overruled all for good. He is certainly a holy, zealous and learned man, besides being a most active man and a business man, though he does not appear such on short acquaintance. These are important advantages."

Archbishop Kenrick made his feelings known to several of his friends and confreres. To a Philadelphia friend he wrote: "I told you, you would have for a bishop one of whom you had never heard or thought. You will love him for your spiritual father he is so full of kindness and so holy."

The Bishop of Natchez said: "I cannot understand how the first named on the list was not appointed."

Archbishop John Hughes of New York, who did not write an opinion to Rome before the appointment, now stated: "I am quite reconciled to the appointment of Father Neumann. . . . I never doubted his merit. But under the actual circumstances I did fear that Philadelphia was not the place for him. But God knows whom to choose and His choice is always the best."

Father Neumann, while these and similar conflicting opinions traveled about, continued quietly with his parish duties, which did not diminish one whit in deference to the imposing event looming ahead. As he went about his routine parish work, Father Neumann was not happy in the thought of the impending consecration. But, as he well knew, the Pope had given him his appointment "under obedience," which meant that he was not free to reject it, or to try to circumvent it.

One group which was enthusiastic about Father Neumann's appointment was the German Catholic population of Baltimore. No doubt the German Catholics in all parts of the country rejoiced, but in Baltimore they did something about it. They contributed a fund for the purchase of the new bishop's episcopal ring, his cross and his crosier.

And so, all preparations having been completed, Father Neumann became the central figure in the crowded church of St. Alphonsus on Passion Sunday in 1852. The new mitre atop his head seemed to accentuate, rather than enhance, his small stature. The glittering cope, or cape, enfolded like a royal garment this little man who wanted no part of the privileges or glamor of royalty. In his left hand he held the crosier, a tall staff which resembled a shepherd's crook, a symbol of his concern for his people.

Previous to the Church ceremony, members of all of the Catholic societies of Baltimore, together with school children, youth groups and parishioners, numbering 1,500, had joined in a parade. With banners flashing in the sunlight, they had marched through the streets, proudly paying tribute to "The Little Bishop," as those who knew and loved him were to call him throughout the trying years ahead.

Who can say what thoughts went through the mind of Father Neumann as his good friend, Archbishop Kenrick, performed the rites of consecration? He must have thought of his family, in far-off Prachatitz. He must have thought first of his mother, who had died three years before. She used to refer to him affectionately as her "little bibliomaniac" when he was studiously reading. Now, it must have brought him a keen sense of sorrow to think that his mother could not be watching her "little bibliomaniac" as he was consecrated a bishop. And yet, to anyone familiar with Father Neumann's staunch faith, it is clear that, in his heart, he knew that she was, indeed, watching him.

And what of his father, Philip Neumann, now approaching the age of 80? As Father Neumann was to learn later, Philip Neumann had his own unique reaction to his son's appointment as bishop. He thought that the report was circulated as a joke.

"Don't bring me such news," he said irritably to the first bearer of the message, flatly rejecting the possibility that it was true.

"Who dares to ridicule us in this way?" he snapped at the next informant.

It wasn't until his son wrote to him that he accepted the truth. And no doubt he marveled at the fact that his son had now progressed to a point where he was one of the leaders of the Catholic Church in America.

Thinking of home, Father Neumann would think fondly of his sisters, particularly Joan, who became a nun. And he would remember, too, his brother, Wenzel (Wenceslaus). Stationed in Detroit as a Redemptorist Brother, Wenzel had permission to make the journey to see Father Neumann consecrated, but he felt that the long journey and the cost involved made it prohibitive. Perhaps he shared his older brother's reluctance to bask in the limelight, even though his status would only be that of the new bishop's brother.

But no one could really discern, watching Father Neumann, what his inner thoughts were as the consecration ceremony progressed. It would have been natural for him to give some thought to his family, and perhaps to remember other birthdays of the long ago. It would have been natural, too, for him to project his ideas forward, and to wonder what problems awaited him in his new office. He seemed to have a dread of his new duties, ever since Archbishop Kenrick's first mention of the possibility that he might become a bishop.

From his outward appearance and conduct, no one would know that he felt any reluctance about assuming the bishopric. But one of his Redemptorist brothers knew exactly what his inner feelings were. To this member of his order he had confided the previous night: "I would rather die than be consecrated tomorrow."

He was probably brought to this state of mind by

thoughts of being caught up again in the vortex of executive activity he had lived in so unhappily during his career as Redemptorist Superior. Apparently he felt this
environment was not the one in which he could do his
best work in the service of God. But God evidently
thought otherwise, since fervent prayers to avoid this
path had not been answered affirmatively. And so, as he
had done before and as he would do again, Father Neumann walked ahead in the path which God had marked
out for him.

The consecration ceremony over, he walked down
the aisle of St. Alphonsus' Church and gave his blessing
to the people. Many of them wept and it was clear that,
although he was leaving them, he would remain in their
hearts.

He delivered his farewell sermon to parishioners
that evening, and those who criticized his speaking manners and efficiency as an orator might well have been
impressed by this address. He spoke in his usual, plain
way, but it was apparent to any observer that he reached
his listeners and held their attention.

He communicated with them, which was not difficult in this case, since he was telling them how much
he regretted leaving them and this he felt very keenly.
He was direct, he was forceful, he was effective, and for
all these reasons his listeners were attentive to his words.
And there was one other ingredient present as he
preached this farewell sermon: His audience was made
up of people who knew him and therefore they heard him
with love.

The German Catholics of the parish came forward
once again in unabashed joy and presented him with a
scroll which put into words the affection they felt for
him. Replying, Bishop Neumann revealed a key to his
character and way of life when he urged them all to have
a strong devotion to the Blessed Virgin, the Mother of

God. This was a lifelong part of his own spiritual armor.

The following day he visited the parochial schools of his parish and bade good-bye to the children, a part of his flock which he loved with great tenderness. In the evening he was once again the center of admiring clergy and parishioners as a crowd gathered at the rectory for the final farewell. His parishioners gave him a purse of $600 and his Redemptorist brothers gave him a gift of $500.

The next day he boarded a train for Philadelphia, accompanied by several of the Redemptorist community. He had with him more money than he had ever had at one time in his life. And this fact was very likely no part of his thoughts as he arrived, on a bleak and dampish day, to take over his duties as the fourth Bishop of Philadelphia.

Father Edward Sourin, a diocesan priest who knew Bishop Neumann's temperament well, had told the bishop's welcomers in Philadelphia that Father Neumann did not like pomp and ceremony and that he would be uncomfortable, albeit affable, as the center of a huge reception crowd. So those in charge of arrangements saw to it that he was greeted quietly and without fanfare.

There was, inevitably, an installation ceremony in the afternoon at St. John's Pro-Cathedral, but this was held with a minimum of accompanying celebration and this comparatively unobtrusive entrance into his new field was very much appreciated by the new bishop. Father Sourin also suggested that Bishop Neumann would be more pleased by the construction of a new school building in the diocese than he would be by any ostentatious welcome. Following through on this suggestion, those in charge announced to the new bishop that a new school would be built, in honor of his coming to serve the diocese. This gave Bishop Neumann a warm glow, and lifted from his heart, at least for the moment, feelings of apprehension and anxiety which had been gnawing at him, now that his new career had moved into the realm of stark reality.

At the close of his first day in Philadelphia, John Neumann slept for the first time in the episcopal residence. It was simply furnished, yet it must have seemed much more comfortable than many of the places in which he had slept since leaving his boyhood home.

Compared to the huts in which he had snatched sleep while making his mission rounds in northern New York, it was palatial. Compared to the various stopping places where he had found surcease from his duties as Redemptorist Superior, it was luxurious. And it was far superior to one other bed in which John Neumann had slept since leaving his boyhood home. That was the bunk aboard the ship *Europa,* the cramped and over-crowded vessel that brought him to the United States sixteen years before.

In a way, his embarking on his new career as bishop was similar to his setting out for this country on the *Europa.* He was moving into new and unknown fields and he was beset by worries and doubts. He must have bestirred himself to try to feel hopeful, just as, before sailing to America, beset by the fear of making the trip alone, he had written in his diary: "But why this fear, as if there were no God?"

And yet, a sense of foreboding would be natural for John Neumann on his first night in Philadelphia. He was tired from a long day of travel and ceremonial receptions. Awaiting him on the morrow were the duties of administering a job which he did not seek and, of his own choice, did not want. It could very well be that he felt some of the vague uncertainty he experienced on his last night aboard the *Europa,* when he penned the lines:

"What is in store for me?"

"What will my future be?"

CHAPTER TWELVE

The city of Philadelphia in the year 1852 was a proud city, rich in historical lore and rich in possessions. The wealthy among the citizenry enjoyed fine standards of living, as befitted their station. The impoverished, as in every large metropolis, struggled along as best they could, their misery somewhat overshadowed to a visitor's gaze by the glitter and pomp of life among the social and intellectual elite.

Significantly, it was to the poor of the diocese that Bishop Neumann gave most of his attention. He seemed to instinctively recoil from the elaborate functions of the well-to-do among his people. He attended these functions, but he was frank in telling his confreres that he preferred the cottages to the mansions.

He seemed to have an intensive drive to seek out people in need of help and a gift for helping them, especially in spiritual matters. When he was making his first tour of his diocese he took time out from his visits to various churches and schools to stop at the county jail. There he talked with two convicted murderers. Their trial had been a sensation in Philadelphia and environs, but Bishop Neumann was not interested in this aspect of their plight. He was concerned about the fact that they were Catholics and that they had rejected spiritual aid and comfort. After he talked with them, they agreed to see a priest, and before they were executed they accepted the kindly ministrations of a priest he sent to them.

Although Bishop Neumann began the tour of his diocese at once, it was some time before he covered it all. The diocese included about half of Pennsylvania, all of Delaware and part of New Jersey. There were 113 parishes, in which a total Catholic population of 170,000 was served by 100 priests. Philadelphia itself, a city of 400,000, contained 90,000 Catholics, more than half of the Catholic population of the diocese.

No doubt in contemplating this vast area and thinking of the many souls under his care, "The Little Bishop" must have been impressed with the scope of his responsibilities. But he did not for a moment turn away from his arduous and complex duties. True, he must have been appalled when, examining the business affairs of the diocese for the first time, he realized that one of his major problems was that harrowing item — church debt.

One can almost hear him say to himself: "Here I am, plunged again into a morass of financial trouble and worry." Thoughts of financial crises in the past no doubt emerged from his subconscious store of unpleasant recollections. And, most harrowing of all his reactions must have been the frustration to his innate urge to help people with their spiritual problems, rather than to give his attention, as he was now obliged to do, to columns of figures, talks of loans and mortgages, and the continuing problem of not wishing to build churches when he had no money. This whole matter was complicated by the necessity to help the immigrants who were coming from Europe in an onrushing tide, seeking financial security and needing also, desperately, spiritual help.

Bishop Neumann realized, of course, that the building of churches was a vital means of helping these people, even though it must have seemed to him less satisfactory and less immediately rewarding than personal

contact with individual souls. Nevertheless he plunged
into his "paper work."

High in priority on his list of problems was the matter of the completion of the cathedral. This imposing edifice, begun by Bishop Kenrick, was heavily in debt and
construction had been halted. Other churches and institutions in the diocese were burdened heavily with debt.
One church, St. Malachy's, was in danger of being sold
by the sheriff.

By temperament, Bishop Neumann could not survey this situation without feeling acute worry. It was almost as though he, personally, owed all of the debts.
And the situation gave him an almost constant feeling of
apprehension. Bishop Kenrick, it should be said, administered his diocese well and improved it a great deal
during his tenure as Bishop. But Bishop Kenrick, Bishop Neumann, and all of the bishops of the United States
at that time were plagued by debts, because they chose
to build and expand to accommodate their immigrant
people, rather than to let these people languish without
spiritual nourishment and perhaps abandon their faith.

The immigration tide was at its flood in these mid-
nineteenth century years and most of the newcomers
were either Irish or German. These people, intent on
finding riches in America, were at times uninterested
and many times unable to contribute substantially to the
church which was going heavily in debt in order to aid
their spiritual welfare. However, the Germans sought to
have their own churches, in which German priests served
them and in which their own language was spoken. This
complicated the situation for Bishop Neumann, who
had a large German population in his diocese.

In spite of difficulties, he tried to give the Germans
their own churches and their own clergy. He even, at one
point, aided a group of Italian Catholics by letting them
use the chapel in his own residence for their services.

Later, he bought a building formerly used as a Protestant church and here St. Mary Magdalen of Pazzi parish was established, the first Italian Catholic parish in the United States.

Bishop Neumann struggled valiantly against the flood of bills, demands from creditors, and other financial hazards. St. Malachy's Church was saved from the auction block after Bishop Neumann called a special meeting and creditors were persuaded to allow the church to continue functioning. He went through worrisome days and weeks and months, hoping and praying that his revenues from his people would increase, at least enough to see him through this emergency period of church development.

He was helped by a unique custom of the times. Catholics were encouraged to lend money to the diocese and many, out of the 170,000 Catholic population of the diocese, were in a position to do this. The money was deposited with an appointed official of the diocese. Receipts were given and the loans were secured by church property. Bishop Neumann was thus, in effect, in the banking business, in the same manner in which other religious groups of the period helped solve their financial problems. It was, as an emergency measure, a help, but it was also "thin ice skating" and indicated the desperate circumstances in which diocesan finances stood at the time.

Happily for him, Bishop Neumann had among his duties the task of making periodic visitations to the outlying areas of his diocese and this gave him opportunity to find a change of pace and respite from the harrowing business of keeping the financial ship afloat. In making these trips he traveled on foot, by train, by stagecoach, or in any fashion that would get him to the nooks and crannies of his far-flung domain.

The journeys took only a few days in some cases. At

other times he might be away for several weeks. Officially, he was obliged to visit every parish every two years.
And he was zealous in traveling to the smallest and most
remote parishes, and visiting every Catholic he could
contact. He was especially interested in meeting Catholics who had lapsed in the practice of their religion.

He said Mass and he heard confessions. He
preached sermons and he administered confirmation.
He visited the sick. He examined the church property
and the parish records. In these visits to small and scattered parishes, far from the pressures of his life in Philadelphia, he found person-to-person contact with people
who needed spiritual help. The trips seemed to revive his
own spirits and they added, penitent sinner by penitent
sinner, to his harvest of souls.

The people welcomed him. In some places, they
staged torchlight parades to mark his coming. He responded with wholehearted love for these people and
they sensed this and received him as one of their own. In
summer sun and winter cold he traveled all over his diocese, to cities, villages, lonely cottages and busy mining
towns. These trips reminded him happily of earlier years
in northern New York where, as a young priest, he journeyed mile after weary mile, buoyed up by the thought
that he was bringing God's charity, forgiveness and love
to hard-working and spiritually hungry people.

In contrast to these rugged journeys Bishop Neumann had the experience, shortly after assuming his
post as bishop, of attending the First Plenary Council of
Baltimore, a gathering of all the bishops and higher officials of the Catholic hierarchy in the United States.
This was an imposing convention, in an atmosphere of
dignity and splendor. There were thirty prelates in attendance. These men held the power to make decisions
and plans which would affect the Catholic Church in
America, not only at that time, but for years to come.

On the opening day of the Council, the assembled prelates marched in procession from the residence of Archbishop Kenrick to the Cathedral. Here was the visual splendor of the American hierarchy and Baltimoreans — both Catholics and Protestants — gathered along the line of march to witness the procession.

Father Michael J. Curley, C.SS.R., in his comprehensive and detailed biography of Bishop Neumann, quotes Robert Joseph Murphy, author of *The Catholic Church in the United States During the Civil War Period,* in giving this picture of the march: "The large cross, the candles of the acolytes, the censers, the long line of surpliced priests, officials and theologians of the Council, the varied robes of the twelve religious orders . . . the rich vestments, the mitres and crosiers of the twenty-four bishops and the six archbishops, with young pages bearing their trains, made a procession of beauty and majesty."

Bishop Neumann was at home in such a gathering. True, the splendor of the procession probably did not suit his taste for the plain and the simple, but, once the Council convened, he took an active part in the deliberations. Inclined to be shy, especially in meeting people for the first time, in this instance he entered into the deliberations of the Council with zeal and enthusiasm, since the assembly was, after all, a vital matter in relation to the well-being of the Church.

His basic scholarship came to the fore. His mastery of several languages helped him to mingle with the prelates, numbering more than one third of the gathering, who came originally from countries where English was not spoken. These men were stationed in frontier localities in this country.

Because of his small stature, Bishop Neumann could not be called, literally, an outstanding figure in the assembly. And yet, in his quiet way, presenting his thoughtful and sincere opinions on subjects discussed, he filled his place with dignity and contributed importantly to the work of the Council.

He served on a committee which dealt with parish schools, a committee which voiced Bishop Neumann's own firm opinion that pastors should establish parochial schools, regardless of whether or not they had support from the State. There had been some State support for parochial schools, but this was being withdrawn in some areas and eventually it was withdrawn altogether. This plea to pastors to develop parochial schools was considered by observers to be the most important matter, in relation to the Church's future in America, that the Council processed.

Bishop Neumann was commissioned by the Council to write a German catechism or submit one current at the time, for the use of the German Catholics. In this way it came about that Bishop Neumann's own catechism received the approval of the Council and was distributed to the German parishes.

An important national problem, on which the Council took no action, was the question of slavery. In this year of 1852 the Civil War was still almost a decade away, but the slavery question was being vehemently discussed and debated all over the country. Some Protestant sects had been divided into Church North and Church South by the intensity of feeling which this subject aroused. Nevertheless, the country as a whole expected that this assembly of all of the important figures in the Catholic Church in America would take a definite. public stand on the issue.

The Council decided not to make any public pronouncement on slavery because any such pronouncement might, in the opinion of the Council members, be construed as taking sides in partisan politics, since political forces were aligned on both sides of the fiery issue.

Also, the subject being a source of bitter argument and debate, the Council members felt that they did not wish to take sides publicly between the advocates of slavery and the abolitionists. Although this decision was a disappointment to many, it did preserve unity in the American Catholic Church.

When the ten-day Council session was over, Bishop Neumann returned to the routine duties of his office, renewing, in his diocesan work, his earlier resolve never to waste a minute, and finding many things to occupy the 1,440 minutes which were his to expend in every day.

His work at the Council won respect and admiration from his confreres among those attending. A Benedictine Abbot subsequently wrote: "At one (or two) Councils of Baltimore . . . I got a chance to discover that he had a really excellent memory and extensive knowledge in theology. He could give an answer to all questions that came up. What edified me most in him was his calmness and self-possession, which proved his humility and self-control. I always did regard him as a little saint!"

"Little Saint," or merely "Little Bishop," John Neumann came back to his diocesan duties determined to implement in his own domain any and all recommendations and directives of the recent Council. The project he was most enthused about was one close to his heart. This was the matter of establishing parochial schools as rapidly as possible.

In fact, just before attending the Council, Bishop Neumann, seeking to speed the establishment of such schools, had organized, on April 28, 1852, a Central Board of Education for his diocese. He was president of this board and was aided by pastors and laymen in carrying out a school building program. There were, of course, many details involved and many problems to be overcome. The most urgent problem was the matter of financing the construction of the buildings.

The establishment of parochial schools was one of the major matters to which Bishop Neumann gave his attention throughout his years as bishop and this effort bore abundant fruit. Word spread to other parts of the country that in Philadelphia genuine progress was being made to increase the number of parish schools.

Out of the Central Board of Education established by Bishop Neumann grew, eventually, the current parochial school system in the United States. Some observers regard Bishop Neumann as "The Father of the Parochial School System." Certain it is that he contributed mightily to this movement in its earliest and most difficult years.

Bishop Neumann's hopes in regard to schools in his diocese are reflected in this excerpt from a letter to his father, written in November of 1853: "Much has been done for the schools. The number of children in them has increased from 500 to 5,000; and before another year has passed, I hope to have 10,000 children in our schools here in Philadelphia."

These beginnings might sound pathetically meager today. And some of the so-called "schools" in some parishes were rather make-shift accommodations; the number of pupils enrolled in many parishes was not large. But Bishop Neumann held to the ideal of having a parochial school in every parish, an adequate building staffed by competent teachers and, with the passing of the years, this dream did come true.

CHAPTER THIRTEEN

In working for the development of the parochial school system Bishop Neumann was motivated, not only by the desire to have Catholic children instructed in their religion, but also by the fact that he was highly critical of the public schools. More than ten years before becoming bishop, he had written to the Archbishop of Vienna that the textbooks used in American public schools at that time presented, in some instances, "malicious perversions of truth and the grossest lies against the doctrine and practices of the Catholic Church."

He also felt very strongly that the irreligious atmosphere of the public schools created a moral climate which was dangerous to the proper development of the children. As one who had mixed and mingled with the people, especially in the country districts, he was in a position to know whereof he spoke.

And so, he pursued his goal of establishing as many parochial schools as he could, in the shortest time, and he also concerned himself with the myriad problems which found their way to his desk. There seemed to be mountains of correspondence demanding his time and demanding his decisions. He would clean up one heap of mail, only to be greeted the following day with a similar load. He did not have a secretarial staff, as is the custom today, but carried on all of his correspondence himself.

Visitors called at the episcopal residence through-

out the day, wanting to see the bishop in regard to matters great and small. He was not of a disposition to turn
anybody away and the visitors took up a great part of his
time. Included among those anxious to see the bishop
were the poor of the diocese. They came with their sad
tales of urgent need, both real and imaginary, and he
helped them all.

He would give them money and, on occasion, he
gave away his own clothes. One of his priests chided him
about his appearance one Sunday and told him that he
looked "shabby." The priest suggested that the bishop
change his clothes and the bishop quietly answered that
he couldn't change his clothes as he had no others.

This charitable impulse to give practical and immediate help to people in need added to the criticism of
"The Little Bishop," who continued to be regarded by
many in the diocese as "not the type" to be Bishop of
Philadelphia.

Father Edward Sourin, whom Bishop Neumann appointed as his vicar-general, said of him: "He knew very
well when he came to this proud city that there were
many, not only among those who differ from us in religion, but hundreds of our own faith who wished as an oc-
cupant for the episcopate of this diocese a man more according to the judgment of the world."

Bishop Neumann ignored all such criticism and
went quietly about his work. A particularly harassing
problem was friction between the Irish and the Germans. He was, as one observer stated, "a German bishop
for the Catholic people in Philadelphia, the great major-
ity of whom were Irish and American."

Bishop Neumann tried to serve both Irish and Germans impartially, but the Germans felt that he should
give them more attention and the Irish felt that he was
favoring the Germans by giving them their own churches
and their own German-speaking priests. He took this

last measure in some desperation, seeking to hold the German Catholics to their faith and apprehensive lest they stray to some sect where dogma might be watered down and greater stress might be placed on social life as they knew it in their native land.

On one particular occasion Bishop Neumann ruled that a new church be built for the English-speaking members of the congregation, who were urgently asking for it, and that, later on, the English-speaking group should help the Germans to build their own church. This plan, adopted by Bishop Neumann after careful consideration of the situation, resulted in serious discord.

The Germans, aroused, said that it was a shame for Bishop Neumann, a German, to desert their cause.

"Thank God I'm not a German; I'm a Bohemian," the bishop told them.

The Germans were so angered at his decision that when he left the town some of them placed a railroad tie across the tracks, to wreck the train on which he rode. The tie was discovered in time and the wreck was prevented, but the Germans were not finished yet with their fight against the bishop's ruling.

They came in a body to the episcopal residence. Here they were voluble and noisy in their protests. Bishop Neumann listened quietly while these rebellious members of his flock went on and on with their protests and recriminations. Then he said the words he felt he had to say: "I excommunicate you!"

The Germans returned home, leaving a saddened bishop to contemplate this revolt by his people. He had tried his best, he had been patient in hearing their angry protests, but he felt that they had gone so far that they left him no choice but to expel them from the Church.

Anxious as he was to gather a harvest of souls, he did not hesitate to use his authority and expel these people from the Church when he felt that their conduct deserved it. Philadelphians who regarded "The Little Bishop" as soft or unequal to the hard tasks of administration learned from this that he would always follow the path he conceived to be the path of duty, no matter how unpleasant for him, no matter how tragic for others.

The rebelling Germans, after he had excommunicated them, realized that he was not to be swayed by noisy demonstrations. They repented of their rebellious conduct and were taken back into the fold.

A look at Bishop Neumann's life shows that he was consistent, letting nothing interfere with his service to God as he saw it. Once one realizes Bishop Neumann's complete dedication to his Creator, his pattern of life becomes a simple one and it is evident that he could never have acted differently in any of the crises which confronted him. True, he was sometimes torn between duty and human considerations, as when he was reluctant to assume the role of bishop, but, in every case, he bowed to God's will and accepted it, no matter what inner torment it caused him.

Although he disliked being involved in money matters, he forced himself to be concerned about the intricacies of the diocese's financial problems, because this was part of his job. On the other hand, when he decided on some activity which promised spiritual help to his people, he found real joy in his work. Thus, when he decided to introduce the Forty Hours Devotion into the diocese on a regular schedule, moving the observance from church to church, he entered into this activity with apostolic zeal.

In this devotion, the Blessed Sacrament is exposed for forty hours on the church altar and the people, praying and meditating before it, address their prayers and petitions to their Sacramental God. The devotion was begun by St. Philip Neri in Rome in the sixteenth century. It had been observed now and then in the Philadel-

phia Diocese and in other sections of the country, but
what Bishop Neumann wished to do was to present it as
a regularly scheduled diocesan activity. He himself had
had a lifelong devotion to the Blessed Sacrament and he
knew what spiritual comfort he received from meditations made in the presence of the Sacred Host and how
often his petitions addressed to Jesus in the Blessed Sacrament had been answered. He was anxious that people
of the diocese be given an opportunity to share in a continuing presentation of this spiritual exercise.

Some of his priests, however, advised against it,
pointing out that anti-Catholic elements in the diocese
had, years before, burned down two churches and that
some of this anti-Catholic feeling was probably still
present. The Know-Nothings, members of a political
group, had shown hostility even to the development of
the parochial schools.

Because of this negative reaction of some of his advisers, and his own uncertainty as to whether or not the
Blessed Sacrament would be safe from scoffers and van-
dals if exposed in a church for forty hours, Bishop Neumann became hesitant about going through with his
plan.

He sat at his desk one night, pondering the question, and he fell asleep, exhausted from the various activities of the day. When he awoke, he noticed that a
candle which had been burning on his desk had ignited
some papers but the papers were not entirely consumed.
He could still read the writing on them. The candle was
still burning. He knelt down to thank God that the fire
had not been a serious one and he seemed to hear the
voice of God saying: "As the flames are burning here
without consuming or injuring the writing, so shall I
pour out My grace in the Blessed Sacrament without
prejudice to My honor. Fear no profanation, therefore;
hesitate no longer to carry out your design for My glory."

Bishop Neumann immediately went ahead with his plans. Very appropriately, the Church of St. Philip Neri was chosen as the site of the first scheduled observance. It began on the Feast of Corpus Christi, 1853, and Bishop Neumann himself spent most of the forty hours in the church with the other worshippers. There was no profanation, no disturbance.

Remarkable results were reported by those who prayed before the Blessed Sacrament during the devotion and the observance moved on to other churches in the diocese. Bishop Neumann himself made up the diocesan schedule.

Today, the Forty Hours Devotion is observed in churches throughout the country, thanks to "The Little Bishop" of Philadelphia and his persistence in organizing and spreading the devotion.

Bishop Neumann was very pleased with the success of the Forty Hours Devotion, but he had no time to spend in any mood of elation. Other pressing problems continued to harass him and one of the most urgent of these was the matter of completing the cathedral. This problem dated back to Archbishop Kenrick's term as bishop. In fact, in various parts of the country at this time, bishops were struggling to complete cathedrals, and the work was being held up for lack of funds.

When Bishop Neumann arrived in Philadelphia, the cathedral consisted of walls, but no roof. Bishop Neumann, with no money for the project, wished to postpone building until he had funds with which to build. But he had something of a reputation among churchmen, and no doubt among laymen, as a builder, because of his building activities before coming to Philadelphia.

And so, criticism of "The Little Bishop" was heard, because the cathedral was not progressing as planned. In particular, there was criticism of the fact that, while needing money for the cathedral's completion, he allowed collections to be taken up by visiting Irish priests for the Catholic University of Ireland. He also allowed collections for other causes. Meanwhile, progress on the cathedral was slow, since funds were low. And, as usual in such projects, even in our own day, the cost was proving to be higher than the estimates.

It seems to have been a part of Bishop Neumann's personality, and a key to his character, that he took upon himself the problems of the diocese in a very intense way, as though he himself were carrying the debt load and the continuing crises as a tangible, physical burden on his shoulders. Perhaps he knew that he could administer the diocese in this way only. Perhaps this was a major reason why he had shied away from the job as bishop.

He continued to make what progress he could with the cathedral, and he continued to build more parochial schools, a project which apparently had priority in his plans, since he would look more to the spiritual activities, rather than to the business of having an imposing edifice as a cathedral.

And then, abruptly, he was confronted with a crisis of major importance. It concerned the "anti-bishop trustees," as they came to be known, at Trinity Church in South Philadelphia.

Bishop Neumann had had some experience with rebellious trustees in the past and the problem with the trustees of Trinity Church was not new. Archbishop Kenrick had had difficulties with this group when he was bishop. The trustees were troublesome and quarrelsome in regard to Kenrick's administration of parish matters and Kenrick sought to have power vested in him as bishop to appoint trustees, rather than elections. When this failed, Kenrick excommunicated several of the trustees. He placed Jesuits in charge of the parish, but the stubborn trustees secured a court injunction, claiming that this transfer of property rights was not legal and the church was closed.

This was the state of affairs when Bishop Neumann arrived in Philadelphia. The problem was like a slow-burning fuse attached to a bomb. No one knew when it might explode and cause havoc.

Bishop Neumann informed the trustees that they would have to surrender the property rights to the church if they wished to have services there. The trustees answered by taking the case to court, to determine whether or not they had legal right to the property.

The full weight of the problem fell on Bishop Neumann's shoulders when the court ruled against him. The trustees were given legal possession of the church.

Bishop Neumann began at once to plan for another church in the area, St. Alphonsus'. The trustees might hold legal possession of the church, but he would not appoint a pastor until loyal trustees were in charge. He also appealed the legal decision to the Supreme Court of Pennsylvania.

This strategy, effective as it appeared to be on the surface, was not really a solution. Bishop Neumann, struggling against mounting debts in the diocese as a whole, was not in a position to take on a new financial obligation. But he felt he had no alternative.

Meanwhile, he had to endure attacks in the press for his conduct of the case. The matter even reached Rome and an archbishop, en route from Rome to Brazil, stopped in Philadelphia to study the problem. The archbishop's study of the case did not lead to its solution; it did increase the mounting tension which Bishop Neumann felt. This tension was further heightened when the bishop was ridiculed in a printed statement which was placed on the desk of every member of the Pennsylvania Legislature. There were charges of despotism and the

Church hierarchy was accused of being arbitrary in using its power.

Through all of this bitter controversy, Bishop Neumann remained silent. He did not issue statements. He did not rant against his attackers. And, at long last, he had his reward. The court decision was in his favor. He, as bishop, was given legal possession of Trinity Church.

The church was reopened and once again developed into a flourishing parish. And so, Bishop Neumann could sit at his desk and contemplate his remaining problems. There seemed to be never a time when he was completely free from some impending crisis, some shadow which threatened to develop into a maelstrom of strife and potential disaster.

But, suddenly, he experienced a great happiness. He had now been Bishop of Philadelphia for more than two years and he had never taken a vacation. Abruptly, or so it must have seemed to "The Little Bishop," he received an invitation from Pope Pius IX to come to Rome and be among those present at the solemn promulgation of the dogma of the Immaculate Conception of the Blessed Virgin Mary.

All of his life Bishop Neumann had a tender devotion to the Mother of God. Here was a summons, in line of duty, to have a part in ceremonies which would honor her before the whole world, and in this prospect he rejoiced. Also, here was an opportunity to visit Rome and to see its beauty and move in its spiritual atmosphere.

For a brief time, he could forget the harassing thoughts about completing the cathedral. He could free his mind of any lingering unpleasantness stemming from the "anti-bishop trustees." He could forget the unending pressures of his daily routine. And he could, before he came back to his episcopal duties, visit his home town of Prachatitz, Bohemia, which he had left long years ago.

He knew his father would welcome him. His relatives and neighbors, his friends from boyhood, would gather at the Neumann home. There would be gaiety, there would be joy, there would be peace.

Looking forward to this, the "strong Bohemian mountain boy," not as strong now as on the day he set out for America, could anticipate a happy time in which he would be able to cast off his cares, his worries, his weariness.

He was going home.

CHAPTER FOURTEEN

Bishop Neumann sailed from the port of New York for Le Havre on October 21, 1854, retracing the route which he had taken to America eighteen years before. This time, he sailed on a steamship, the *Union,* a happy contrast to the overcrowded sailing ship, the *Europa,* on which he had made his first voyage.

As on his first voyage, Bishop Neumann kept to himself a great part of the time. No doubt he was grateful for time which he could now spend in reading and in contemplation. His spiritual life, while he served as bishop, was often crowded into the background by his concern with immediate problems in his diocese.

The trip was a stormy one. The *Union* was lashed by wind and wave, part of the ferocious storm pattern which, in the year 1854, brought death and destruction to many ships traveling the Atlantic. However, the *Union* was faster and sturdier than the *Europa,* which had taken forty days for its journey. In just seventeen days after leaving New York the *Union* arrived at Le Havre.

Bishop Neumann's thoughts must have gone back to the young John Neumann who set out for America from Le Havre eighteen years before. He was then only twenty-five years old, eager and anxious to spend his life in the service of God. He had not even been ordained. He was taking what might be regarded as a gamble for the glory of God, a gamble which, thus far at least, he had won.

Arriving in Paris the day after the *Union* docked at Le Havre, Bishop Neumann wrote to his father, telling him that, after his visit to Rome, he would be coming home. Then he proceeded to Marseilles by train, across the Mediterranean to Civita Vecchia and to Rome.

In the Eternal City Bishop Neumann was a guest at a Redemptorist community. Apparently, this suited his mood exactly. He dressed in a Redemptorist habit and wore no insignia to mark his rank as a bishop. He traveled about Rome on foot, making the traditional pilgrimage of seven churches several times and celebrating Mass at the city's historic shrines.

His fellow members of the Redemptorist Order noted his humility, his piety and his quiet, peaceful attitude. Obviously, he was enthralled at being on the site of so much of the Catholic Church's history. One of the churches where he celebrated Mass was St. Mary Major, which contains relics of the Holy Crib and which also holds the tomb of St. Pius V.

Moving about Rome, his mind free of the pressure of his diocesan problems, Bishop Neumann must have experienced a spiritual joy such as he had never known before. Here were constant reminders of Christ's life on earth and of the strength and vigor of His Church. Here, in churches, at shrines, and in the very atmosphere of the city, was the whole dramatic and colorful story of the Catholic Church's early martyrdom and later triumph.

And Bishop Neumann was no doubt thrilled by the thought that he himself, within a few days, was to be an eyewitness at an historic event in Church history. Every day members of the hierarchy were arriving in Rome from all parts of the world. When all were assembled, this distinguished gathering numbered more than 150.

Bishop Neumann spent quite a bit of his time with

these churchmen at meetings relating to the forthcoming event. The Pope presided at a gathering of all the visiting prelates. Finally, the preparations completed, December 8 was selected as the date for the definition of the dogma of the Immaculate Conception.

On that day the whole city seemed to hold an air of excitement. The more than 150 prelates, together with thousands of priests, members of religious orders and the laity, were in attendance at St. Peter's, where the Pope celebrated a Pontifical High Mass. During the ceremony the Dean of the Sacred College asked the Pope to define infallibly the doctrine of the Immaculate Conception of the Blessed Virgin Mary.

The Pope, acceding to the request, prayed to the Holy Spirit and the entire congregation joined in the prayer. Then came the Pope's solemn words: "We declare, pronounce and define that the doctrine which holds that the Blessed Virgin Mary in the first moment of her conception by the singular favor and privilege of Almighty God in view of the merits of Jesus Christ, the Savior of the human race, was preserved immune from all stain of original guilt, has been revealed by God and therefore must be firmly and constantly believed by all the faithful."

That night, there was a festive atmosphere in the city of Rome. St. Peter's and other historic buildings were illuminated and a glow of light seemed to bathe the whole city. Streets and highways were crowded with pedestrians and carriages as the entire populace joined in manifesting their joy at the historic event.

Bishop Neumann's reaction was contained in a letter to a friend. "I thank the Lord God that among the many graces He has bestowed upon me, He allowed me to see this day in Rome," he wrote.

Before he left the Eternal City Bishop Neumann reported to the Pope on the condition of his diocese. As a bishop, he was required to make what is called an *ad limina* visit to the Pope periodically, reporting on diocesan affairs, and his visit to Rome gave him the opportunity to do this.

The bishop was able to point out, as a highlight of his report, that there were now thirty-four parochial schools in his diocese and that the number of pupils was close to 9,000. This was not far short of the figure of 10,000 pupils which he had hopefully predicted a year before, in a letter to his father.

He also told the Pope that there was urgent need for an orphan asylum in his diocese to take care of the children of deceased German immigrants. The result of his concern for these children was the establishment of a branch of the Franciscan Sisters, who administered the orphanage and subsequently grew into a large and busy community whose good works were widespread.

It was now time for Bishop Neumann to plan for his visit home and so he moved overland through Italy, Austria and on to Bohemia, the country we know today as Czechoslovakia. En route, he encountered difficulties. He still wore no insignia to mark him as a bishop and he appeared to be a priest. When an Austrian official demanded his passports he produced them, but the official apparently could not read his credentials, written in English, and he was marched to the local police station. After he produced his episcopal cross and identified himself, he was released.

At another time, he lost a collection of relics which he had brought from Rome and other places on his itinerary. Inquiries about the valuable package brought no word of its whereabouts. Like many another person worried about the return of lost articles, Bishop Neumann turned to St. Anthony, promising to say his next Mass in the saint's honor and to initiate special services in his honor in one of the Philadelphia churches if the relics were found. Almost immediately a youth appeared and said, "Bishop, here is your lost package."

Continuing his journey, Bishop Neumann stopped at several Redemptorist houses. These were stopovers which he thoroughly enjoyed. His confreres always made him welcome and he always felt at home with them. In the course of his travels he met his old friend, Adalbert Schmidt, his fellow seminarian of years ago. Adalbert, as a seminarian, had shared John Neumann's dream of being a missionary in America. Later, he changed his plans and was now the director of a seminary. They revived their earlier friendship and no doubt felt young and happy as they relived, if only momentarily, their vanished youth.

At Prague, Bishop Neumann was the dinner guest of ex-Emperor Ferdinand who, in addition to being a gracious host, gave the bishop a substantial donation for his diocese. Bishop Neumann, as in Philadelphia, did not care particularly for the glitter and pomp of the formal dinner, but he was grateful for the gift. He knew many uses for it in Philadelphia.

Also in Prague, a highlight of Bishop Neumann's travels was a visit with his sister, Joan, who was Superior at the motherhouse of the Sisters of St. Charles. This was the first tangible link with home and one can imagine how brother and sister enjoyed this meeting and how it brought back memories.

In Budweis, Bishop Neumann visited the seminary where he had prepared for his vocation. Here he met John Berger, the son of his sister Catherine, and together they drove towards Prachatitz in a sleigh. Once again Bishop Neumann was seeing one of the white winters he knew as a child, with snow blanketing the countryside, the air bracingly cold, and sleighs being used as the common means of travel.

Bishop Neumann wished to make a very quiet entrance into Prachatitz, just as, when appointed bishop, he wished to make a quiet entrance into Philadelphia. But, this time, his modest plans were not to be executed. As he and John Berger approached the town of Nettolitz, near Prachatitz, church bells started to ring and people rushed from their homes to bid the bishop welcome. So sincere was their emotion that Bishop Neumann was persuaded to stay in Nettolitz overnight.

John Berger, who later became a Redemptorist, wrote a biography of Bishop Neumann, and in it many details about his career have been preserved. John Berger tells us that, in Nettolitz, Bishop Neumann pleaded with him, "Let's send the sleigh back to Budweis and walk into Prachatitz by the back road. It's only three hours and I know the way. I walked it many times as a student."

When it came time to leave Nettolitz the next day, the sleigh was gone, but in its place was a sleigh drawn by four horses and presided over by a coachman in livery. It was the private sleigh of Prince Schwartzenberg. It must have been at about this time that Bishop Neumann realized he was a prisoner, a prisoner of these warmhearted people who would insist on showering him with the welcome they felt he deserved. In Philadelphia, he was "not the type" to be bishop, in the minds of many of his people, but in his home town and environs he was a neighbor, a celebrity and a hero, and from the love and devotion of these people there was no escape.

His departure from Budweis had been reported along the route by a "spy" assigned to watch his movements. The people of Prachatitz had ample time to prepare their welcome.

As the sleigh drew near to Prachatitz crowds of cheering people lined the highway, standing in the snow and ignoring the biting cold. A band blared forth its message of welcome. Bells rang and guns were fired in salute. Passing through the gates of his home town, Bishop Neumann, the reluctant central figure in this awesome din, saw armed guards standing at salute and saw his own coat of arms proudly displayed.

He stopped at the village church, while a happy crowd surrounded him. Inside the little church where he had served as altar boy, where he had prayed for light when he first felt the call to the service of God, Bishop Neumann, with the crowd waiting outside, prayed silently. Then he rose from his knees, rejoined the throng, and walked with them to his home, not far away.

He saw his father, now eighty years old, standing in front of the house, his arms outstretched in welcome. And as John Neumann approached, his father gathered "The Little Bishop" into his arms and carried him inside. This was Philip Neumann's eloquent way of saying, without words, that he was proud of his son, that he loved him, and that he was overjoyed to have him home.

Philip Neumann carried "The Little Bishop" into the living room and set him down before the admiring gaze of neighbors and friends. Here were the old rooms, the old familiar scenes. His sister Louise was the only one of the six Neumann children now at home. But surely, in his mind's eye, and in his heart, Bishop Neumann must have seen them all.

"Too bad his mother is not here," a thoughtless member of the crowd remarked.

"Mother is happy, looking down on us today," Bishop Neumann said.

For a full week Bishop Neumann knew the happiness of being once again with his loved ones, his family and his neighbors. To a man who preferred to go his way without fanfare or fuss, all this show of affection must have been distracting, but he accepted it gratefully, knowing that these people were displaying emotion which they felt deeply. His reaction might well be illustrated by a remark he made when he first experienced the exuberant welcome at Nettolitz, "God forgive these people for tempting me to vanity."

But there is no doubt that he enjoyed his visit. He said Mass every day at the village church and crowds came to attend the Masses. They continued to visit the Neumann home, all seeking his blessing, and he responded with friendliness, humility and mildness. He had time and opportunity to talk with his father and his sister Louise of days gone by. He had time and opportunity to retrace the shortcut he used to take from his home to school. And he had time and opportunity to recall vividly a memory of his mother. He could almost see her, sitting in her chair by a window, distributing food and alms to the poor of the village as she was accustomed to do one day each week.

On a sunny and cold afternoon he walked to his mother's grave. He knelt in the snow and thanked God for giving him this mother who, in her loving way, directed his steps to his vocation. "Mother is happy, looking down on us today," he had told his neighbors. He must have felt certain that his mother was in heaven, for the simple reason that he knew his mother. He knew her kindness and her charity and, like many a man kneeling at the grave of the woman who bore and nurtured him, he could not imagine God being angry with his mother. And she, looking down on her "little bibliomaniac," must have felt a mother's pride in all he had done and all he was to do.

When it was time to leave Prachatitz, Bishop Neumann left quietly, before daybreak, without noisy farewells, and perhaps this was best. A priest who was with him tells the story that as Bishop Neumann looked for the last time at his home town, tears coursed down his cheeks. Perhaps it was best that the people of Prachatitz

remembered him in the happy mood in which he had enjoyed his visit home.

En route to Paris and sailing he stopped at Munich
and was persuaded to sit for a portrait. He had declined
several times in the past to do this, pleading that he was
not an important personage, but this time he was persuaded by the plea that proceeds from the sale of the
portrait would be given to the poor of Prachatitz. And so
today there is a single portrait of John Neumann as a
bishop.

At Paris he learned that there would be a two-week
delay before a sailing to New York, so he hurried to
Liverpool and sailed on the *Atlantic*. Again it was a
stormy voyage, but again it was a seventeen-day voyage,
as compared to his forty-day trip on the *Europa*. Aside
from the comparative speed of the *Atlantic*, there were
other factors which made the bishop's second voyage to
America a more comfortable one. On his first voyage,
provisions on board were low in the final days of the trip;
the drinking water had worms in it; the passengers, some
of them ill, were bickering and quarreling, their nerves
taut and strained by the long trip.

No such unpleasantness marred the trip on the
Atlantic and Bishop Neumann must have enjoyed this
quiet interlude before again assuming his duties in
Philadelphia. He was rested and refreshed. He was looking forward to telling his people of his experiences and to
urging them to pray to the Mother of God under the title
of the Immaculate Conception.

The *Atlantic* docked at New York on March 28,
1855. March 28 was an important date in the life of "The
Little Bishop." It was his forty-fourth birthday and the
third anniversary of his consecration as a bishop. As he
disembarked from the *Atlantic* he bore no resemblance
to the young John Neumann who, nineteen years before,
had landed in New York. The young John Neumann had

shabby clothes, worn shoes, money which would total less than a dollar in American coin, and no definite destination.

And there was one other way in which Bishop Neumann stood in sharp contrast to his younger self. The young John Neumann landed in America without a hat. It had been stolen on shipboard. Bishop John Neumann, of course, had a hat. And he also had, among his possessions, another very important and symbolic hat. He had a bishop's mitre.

The mitre, or at least the responsibility it represented, must have been very much in his thoughts as he entrained for Philadelphia. He knew he was returning to vexing financial problems and complex administrative chores. But after his absence of almost half a year he must have felt fit and ready to assume his episcopal duties.

He had no way of knowing, of course, that the next few years would bring him the most trying burdens of his career.

CHAPTER FIFTEEN

One of Bishop Neumann's first official acts on returning to his diocese was to issue a pastoral letter on the subject of the Immaculate Conception. He urged all of the pastors of the diocese to hold triduums in their churches, in honor of the Mother of God.

The pastors responded with enthusiasm. Throughout the diocese these three-day services attracted thousands of parishioners. Their spiritual activity no doubt brought joy to the heart of Bishop Neumann. The observance was an echo of his trip to Rome and it focused attention on the Virgin Mary, to whom he always had a strong devotion.

In such spiritual activity he found peace, and surcease from less pleasant chores. But then he had to turn again to diocesan problems. And the diocesan problems, in that year of 1855, were not pleasant to contemplate. A wave of anti-Catholic feeling was sweeping the country. The Know-Nothings, a political group so called because members professed ignorance of what went on at their meetings, were actively working against Catholics.

The heart of their attitude was expressed in this party plank adopted at their national convention: "Resistance to the aggressive policy and corrupting tendency of the Roman Church in our country by the advancement to all political stations — legislative, executive, judicial and diplomatic — of only those who do not hold civil allegiance to any foreign power, civil or ecclesiastical, and who are Americans by birth, education and training, thus fulfilling the maxim that Americans only shall govern America."

This anti-Catholic feeling was probably increased by the emergence of prominent Catholics into the country's public life. President Franklin Pierce appointed a Philadelphia Catholic, James Campbell, as Postmaster General and this stirred up the "nativists," as the anti-Catholic forces were called. A Massachusetts Congressman charged that, according to Catholic belief, "the Pope is Supreme not only in matters of Faith but also has a temporal power that can not only control governments, but, in fitting exigencies, may absolve his disciple from his allegiance."

In our own day, such an anti-Catholic attitude would not be taken seriously. The injustice of it was exposed and the charge itself repudiated in the successful presidential campaign of the late John F. Kennedy. But, in the 1850s, such charges fed the flames of anti-Catholicism.

In the State of Maine a priest was tarred and feathered. In Massachusetts, the legislature appointed a committee to inspect convents. In Kentucky, during an attack on Catholics, homes were burned and twenty persons lost their lives.

In Philadelphia, the anti-Catholic activists did not resort to violence, but when Bishop Neumann returned from Rome he found that the "nativists" and their supporters were in political control in Philadelphia and their influence gave them decisive power in state politics. Bishop Neumann, being both a Catholic and a foreigner, came under sharp attack by flamboyant orators and the printed word.

These personal attacks he could ignore, as was his habit, but the anti-Catholic forces scored a tangible

triumph when the Pennsylvania Legislature, by an overwhelming vote, passed the Price Bill. This document,
named for the legislator who sponsored it, prevented
bishops from handing down to their successors the title
to church property. It also provided that lay members of
the parish be in control of church property. In other
words, the bishops were simply holding church property
in trust for their congregations. This played directly into
the hands of church trustees, with whom Bishop Neumann had already had unpleasant experiences. Under
the Price Bill, if the trustees rebelled against a bishop's
ruling, the bishop could not claim the church property;
by state law, it belonged to the congregations.

As part of their attack, the "nativists" tried to show
the bishops as being anxious to acquire property in their
own names in order to become wealthy. They referred to
the bishops derisively as "Prince Bishops." This accusa-
tion was particularly absurd in the case of Bishop Neumann. His abstemious way of living and his love of poverty were known to all of his people.

"In reality he is not personally worth a dollar," one
of his supporters wrote. "If rich in anything, it is in debts
and toils and manifold cares which he knew would be his
estate from the hour when, believing it to be heaven's
will, he consented to wear a crown of thorns in the shape
of a mitre."

To add to Bishop Neumann's unrest, an economic
depression had set in and a wave of unemployment
swept the diocese. Soup kitchens were opened in Philadelphia to feed the hungry. In the minds of many of the
unemployed, the matter of contributing to church support was understandably displaced by the necessity of
providing food for the family.

And, as a continuing problem, Bishop Neumann
was still a bishop without a cathedral. There was a chapel in the episcopal residence but it was badly overcrowd-

ed each Sunday. Plan after plan to increase donations to the Cathedral Building Fund were tried, none of them successful. A drive to get the roof on the cathedral before the end of 1855 met with failure. The situation seemed, to Bishop Neumann's critics, to indicate that he was inefficient in raising funds and the roofless cathedral loomed like a symbol of the financial insecurity of the whole diocese.

During all of the travail he experienced in trying to keep the diocese from financial ruin, Bishop Neumann continued to make his visitations to outlying parishes. This was a spiritual activity he loved. He spent five months of each year on these trips. It seemed to refresh him to make a jaunt into some little town and administer to the spiritual wants of the people, quietly fulfilling his episcopal duty and quietly adding to his harvest of souls.

No sacrifice of time or personal comfort persuaded him to overlook any obscure territory, or any single soul in need of aid. On one trip he was informed that a boy who lived in a remote spot in the Allegheny Mountains wished to be confirmed. He traveled a whole day to the practically inaccessible spot and confirmed the child. To someone who remonstrated that he was imposing hardship on himself he answered: "Has not that child a soul to be saved?"

This was the pattern of his harvest. He would do whatever was necessary to give spiritual aid to his people. One day he arrived at a small town and began to hear confessions. He soon realized that the people spoke Gaelic and many of them couldn't make their confessions in English. This troubled Bishop Neumann, who was accustomed to spending long hours in the confessional and who knew what peace confession could bring to penitent souls. When he returned to Philadelphia he took up the study of Gaelic. As a linguist, familiar with several languages, he was able to learn Gaelic quickly. On his next visitation tour, he heard confessions in that particular town in Gaelic as well as English. The people responded with deep gratitude and appreciation. One old lady said: "Thanks be to God, we have an Irish bishop!"

In other spiritual activities he also displayed his zeal and keen interest in the development of the diocese. When a mission was given at the cathedral, he appeared each morning at five o'clock, to help out in any way that he could. When not on visitations, he tried to spend one day each month as a day of recollection. He would spend these days with the Redemptorist priests at St. Peter's in Philadelphia. His attitude was quiet and self-effacing. He would allow no special privileges for himself because of his episcopal rank. Many times he joined with his confreres in washing dishes, this being a recommendation to superiors in the Redemptorist rule. The simplicity of his attitude in regard to the welfare of the diocese is revealed in this excerpt from a letter he wrote to a nun: "I pray each day to the Holy Spirit to give me the light necessary for the good of my diocese, and I hope that my prayers will not be in vain."

A project to which he devoted much thought and time was the bringing of religious orders into the diocese, to serve as teachers and to work in the hospitals, orphanages, and other institutions. He himself established the Sisters of the Third Order of St. Francis of Glen Riddle, a group whose good works through the years are incalculable. He also established a preparatory seminary for the education of young boys.

His attitude toward the priests and religious under his care was one of tenderness and solicitude. The story is told that he once visited a convent which was in dire and immediate need of financial help. He evidently came prepared. When one of the nuns outlined their problems in getting even sufficient food, "The Little Bishop" spoke some encouraging words. He then referred to his custom of frequently distributing medals. "And now," he said, "I'm going to give you some Yankee medals." From his pocket he took fifty dollars in gold pieces and gave them to the nuns to tide them over their emergency.

In all such activities, Bishop Neumann seemed to be a happy administrator, molding his diocese and his people into the ideal community he envisaged. It was only when he returned to the task of administration on the business or financial level that he seemed to feel a great inadequacy and frustration.

The Bishop of Pittsburgh summed up the situation with these words: "It is known that when he returns from a visitation of his diocese, he is accustomed to say that he feels like a man, as it were, being led to the gallows."

Typical of the kind of diocesan developments which filled him with a sense of defeat and failure was the matter of St. Alphonsus' Church. Construction of this church was begun when Holy Trinity Church was closed because of trouble with the trustees. When the trouble was resolved by the courts Holy Trinity Church was reopened and many parishioners returned to worship there. So, as a consequence, the congregation of St. Alphonsus' Church dwindled and so did the anticipated revenue. Things reached a point where St. Alphonsus' Church was in dire straits, so heavily in debt that drastic action was needed. Bishop Neumann solved the problem, at least temporarily, with loans from his people and by emergency collections throughout the diocese. But there was criticism of the bishop for building St. Alphonsus' Church on too large a scale and therefore being inept in matters involving expenditures.

Again, he faced criticism when he purchased land

for the construction of a school, and it later developed, after the school was built, that the use of the land for a public school was forbidden under terms of the original deed. This matter was later resolved in the courts and the school was opened. But, in the meantime, some people were quick to say that Bishop Neumann was a failure in financial transactions.

At another time he was offered land for an orphanage. Money for the purchase of the land was to be donated by a wealthy benefactor. But the wealthy benefactor suffered serious financial losses, due to a fire, and he was unable to aid Bishop Neumann as he had promised. Bishop Neumann purchased the land for the orphanage and struggled along with the expenditure as best he could. Here again there was criticism of "The Little Bishop" as being inadequate in his job.

Out of such experiences, Bishop Neumann developed a strong feeling of dissatisfaction with himself. The thought weighed heavily on him and he devoted much thought and prayer to seeking a solution. It was his custom at this time to spend many hours in prayer, usually during the night.

Some of his confreres wondered if he took time out for a good night's rest. According to the record, he did not. His nephew, John Berger, wrote in a letter home, "For many years he slept scarcely one hour at night." This seems like an exaggeration, but the consensus is that he slept little. Those who observed him during his term as bishop have said that he often slept on the floor of his room, rather than in his bed. Many times he slept in his chair.

In the matter of food, he seemed at times almost indifferent to it. In the morning, although he had a bell in his room and could summon his housekeeper to bring him coffee or whatever he wished, he never used it. His breakfast consisted of coffee alone. And he would go without it if no one was in the dining room at the moment he appeared.

This abstemious way of living, apparently followed in the spirit of mortification, might lead some folks to think that the bishop was troubled by scrupulosity. But Father Francis X. Tschenhens, his confessor and the man who knew him best, has said that Bishop Neumann was too humble to be scrupulous. His whole attitude towards his God and his duties as a bishop could be summed up in two words, which he himself often used: "Soli Deo!" . . . "For God Alone!"

Out of his feelings of inadequacy and frustration, Bishop Neumann emerged, in May of 1855, with a solution, a solution which was to startle not only his confreres but all of the people of his diocese and was to be echoed in Rome. At the Eighth Provincial Council of Baltimore he asked that the Diocese of Philadelphia be divided in two, and that he as bishop be given the less important of the two segments. It is significant to note that nobody had suggested this step until Bishop Neumann made his proposal. The action was entirely voluntary on his part.

The prelates at the Council, somewhat stunned by the bishop's proposal, discussed it at some length. There were good reasons to consider the division of the diocese. It was very large and it was growing. The assembled bishops were in favor of dividing the diocese.

Whether or not Bishop Neumann would remain in Philadelphia was a decision which the bishops left to the Church authorities in Rome. The bishops sent to Rome the names of three priests recommended as their choices for the See of Pottsville, suggested as the site of the new bishopric. They also sent three names as recommendations for the See of Philadelphia, in the event that the Pope decided to grant Bishop Neumann's request that he be bishop of the less important of the two divisions.

There the matter rested when the Council came to a close.

Two weeks later Bishop Neumann wrote to the Secretary of the Sacred Congregation in Rome: "I manifested to the Fathers my desire to be named to another See where I would not be overwhelmed with financial transactions, for which I find myself daily less equal, both on account of my way of life and the habits of my mind which abhor such things, and on account of the great fear I have that the financial affairs of the diocese might suffer greatly unless they are entrusted to hands more skillful than mine. . . .

"I have always loved the labors of a missionary, travels, visitations, the heat of the summer and the cold of winter and the like. I have even sought them, but I have a horror of debts and financial transactions. . . . Because of my poor talents and lack of insight, I commit mistakes especially in the administration of temporal matters, and I fear these will involve me and my successors in greater difficulties and obligations which they will be unable to remedy.

"It must be clear to you that a bishop of such a great diocese should be a man who shines by his authority, who is prudent in taking counsel and most strong in carrying things through. Although I endeavor sincerely to fulfill all the obligations of my office, it daily becomes more sure and clear to me that I cannot, without presuming to tempt God, expect that all things will advance prosperously in the future.

"I beseech you not to take this declaration of mine as an expression of humility. Before God it is the truth which I have thought should be manifested to those whose office it is to care for the welfare of this diocese. . . ."

CHAPTER SIXTEEN

Shortly after he wrote to Rome, Bishop Neumann wrote to his friend Archbishop Kenrick, telling him the gist of his message to Rome and stating that he would feel at home in either Pottsville, Pennsylvania, or Wilmington, North Carolina.

"I really think before God that Wilmington would be the very place for me," he wrote. "As there may be some difficulty, if not an impossibility, to find a priest willing to go to Wilmington, my prospect is brighter of finding there the desired *otium cum dignitate*. I fear, however, that they will regard my protestations and statements as nothing but a fine display of very praiseworthy or crooked humility, and leave me splashing in the midst of my floating and non-floating debts."

Archbishop Kenrick was quick to reply to Bishop Neumann, advising him to leave the resolution of his problem in the hands of God and, meanwhile, to continue with his job. The bishop, of course, had been leaving the resolution of his problems in the hands of God all his life, but in this crisis he felt a natural anxiety as to what, and where, his future would be.

From the Secretary of the Sacred Congregation in Rome, he received word that his request for a less important see than Philadelphia would be taken under consideration. But no encouragement for Bishop Neumann's request was offered.

"I do not believe that the petition to leave Philadelphia can be readily admitted," the letter read. "The Sacred Congregation well knows with what solicitude you rule the Diocese of Philadelphia and, though excellent names are sent for that place, very great inconveniences might result from a change of this nature."

Thus, Bishop Neumann was left with feelings of doubt and uncertainty as to his future, or left, to quote his own words, "splashing in the midst of my floating and non-floating debts."

Archbishop Kenrick wrote to the Cardinal Prefect of Propaganda, setting forth his own appraisal of Bishop Neumann: "It seems to me that he should by all means be retained in the See of Philadelphia, since he is a shining light because of his piety and his labors. I, indeed, confess that he is wanting a little in managing affairs, but I believe that he can appoint a vicar general, consultors and helpers, whose assistance will enable him to clear the debts and smooth out matters. He is beloved by the clergy and people, although certain ones would like to see more urbane and polished manners."

The feeling of these critics was not that Bishop Neumann did not have good manners, but that he did not follow the modes of the day.

The Bishop of Pittsburgh, who had registered opposition to Bishop Neumann's appointment as bishop, wrote to authorities in Rome: "Much as I dislike writing about this, still I cannot but indicate some facts which may influence the Sacred Congregation. The Bishop of Philadelphia is a man conspicuous for zeal and sanctity, and in the performance of his sacred duty he has effected very much good. But he is very timid, is not so well versed in the language as to be able to address the people effectively; his manners are inclined to keep him aloof from the clergy and the people, and therefore there is no love or affection toward him."

In the center between these conflicting views, Bishop Neumann continued with his routine of diocesan duties. As he did so, he must have more than once recalled the words he had written to the Prefect of Propaganda: "Would that a merciful decision may very soon be made regarding me, for I am in great distress here, passing my days and nights without sleep and filled with affliction of spirit."

Those who thought that Bishop Neumann was not beloved by his people were not close enough to him to make an accurate judgment. They were not with him, for example, on the day that he brought a three-year-old girl from St. Vincent's Home in Philadelphia to an orphan asylum some distance away. The child was sick and throughout the journey Bishop Neumann took care of her so solicitously that she always referred to him thereafter as "my priest."

And they were not with him in the episcopal residence the day two little girls came to bring him a message from the Sisters of the Holy Cross. While they waited in the parlor for the bishop, they gazed in admiration at a marble statue of a child in a cradle. Coming into the parlor, Bishop Neumann noticed their absorption in the statue and good-humoredly told them that he would give the statue to the little girl who could carry it home. The girls each tried to lift the statue and failed. But one of them returned with a small wagon, to carry the statue. Bishop Neumann was so touched by this that he let the little girl take the statue. This girl, Margaret McSheffery, later entered the convent and served as Mother General of the Holy Cross Sisters. The statue became a treasured possession of the order.

And those who thought Bishop Neumann was not beloved by his people were never in the episcopal rectory when the poor of Philadelphia came asking for help. True, some of the poor must have regarded "The Little

Bishop" as a "soft touch," and used the money he gave them for any frivolity they had in mind. He must have known that some of them took advantage of his charity. But he turned no one away. Once when his housekeeper told him that a certain woman was a "repeater," coming back a second time, he answered simply that her need must be great if she asked twice for help.

He preferred the homes of the poor to those of the rich. A priest who accompanied him on a visitation tour related that one evening they were dinner guests in a log cabin. "What a difference between yesterday and today," Bishop Neumann later remarked. "Yesterday we were treated to a well-filled table, empty forms of politeness and useless conversation, but today we had the charming simplicity of a pious Catholic home." Archbishop Kenrick summed up this attitude of Bishop Neumann with the words: "He was father to the poor, the humble and the lowly. He shrank as it were from contact with the rich."

As Bishop Neumann awaited word from Rome on his future, the days went by, the weeks went by, and the months.

During this time tragedy struck in one of the Philadelphia parishes. The people of St. Michael's parish had planned a picnic. The date was July 17, 1856. In a gala mood parents and children boarded a train and set out for the country. A similar affair a year previously had been a big success and the group was looking forward to another happy day and more happy memories.

The departure from Philadelphia was a bit late and the engineer, speeding along a single track, was trying to make up lost time. He had to get his train onto a side switch, enabling another scheduled train to come through on the single track from the opposite direction. He was too late. The other train came into sight and the two trains crashed head-on. Sixty-five of the picnickers were killed and many more injured.

Bishop Neumann heard of the tragedy while he was out in the country on a visitation tour. He hurried back to Philadelphia and visited the hospitals where the injured were being treated. He administered the sacraments and gave what comfort he could to the hundreds whose bright dream of a holiday had ended in disaster. This tragedy, naturally, added to his burden as he moved through day after frustrating day, doing his best to deal with diocesan problems.

Finally, on March 30, 1857, Archbishop Kenrick received official word from Rome that Bishop Neumann was to be given a coadjutor to aid in administering the diocesan affairs. The coadjutor, one of the three men suggested as Bishop of Philadelphia at the Eighth Council of Baltimore if Bishop Neumann were transferred, was Father James Frederick Wood. He was consecrated Bishop and took up his new duties at once.

James Frederick Wood was a brilliant man. He was a convert who had spent years in the banking business before becoming a priest and he was particularly qualified to help Bishop Neumann with financial problems, and to administer diocesan affairs whenever Bishop Neumann was out of Philadelphia on his visitation rounds. Bishop Neumann welcomed him with joy.

Bishop Wood was a suave, sophisticated type. His personality was outgoing and demonstrative, as compared to Bishop Neumann's habitually quiet manner. He was a tall man and made a strong impression on any gathering he attended. He had an interest in attending social functions which Bishop Neumann lacked. For the moment, it appeared that peace and quiet had descended on the Diocese of Philadelphia.

Then, suddenly, the historic and devastating Panic of 1857 swept the country. Philadelphia, like all other cities, felt its crippling lash. Businesses went bankrupt, manufacturing practically ceased, and the common man, the most pathetic victim of all depressions and panics, walked the streets in a despairing rhythm which echoed his condition . . . unemployed . . . unemployed . . . unemployed.

People who had loaned their money to the Philadelphia Diocese rushed to reclaim it and Bishop Wood found himself the target of this crucial threat to the diocesan finances. Fortunately, after the first rush, the people came to the conclusion that they would rather have their money in diocesan hands than in the banks, and so the diocesan funds weathered the storm.

Bishop Neumann and Bishop Wood worked well together. The only element of dissatisfaction came from the fact that Bishop Wood seems to have had the idea that Bishop Neumann was soon to leave Philadelphia and that he, Bishop Wood, would step into the ruling role. This was a misunderstanding of the situation, but in his letters to friends, Bishop Wood indicated that this was his expectation. Bishop Neumann, on the other hand, accepted the coming of Bishop Wood gratefully and, in the new circumstances, enjoyed comparative peace and tranquillity.

There came a happy day when the cathedral funds finally reached a point where a roof could be placed over the edifice. This was a joyful event for Bishop Neumann, after years of struggle. The inside of the cathedral would not be completed for several years, but at long last the cathedral had a roof and its symbolism, accentuating the precarious financial condition of the diocese, was changed to one of progress and hope.

On the Feast of the Exaltation of the Holy Cross, September 14, 1859, a gold cross was placed on the cathedral dome. It was a day of rejoicing, for Bishop Neumann and for all of his clergy and people who had contributed money, time and effort to advance the work. Thousands of people attended the ceremonies. There was a solemn procession from the episcopal residence to the cathedral, where Bishop Martin John Spalding of Louisville spoke on "The Significance of the Cross." He was a gifted orator and he left with the huge assembly the thought that "our true Fatherland is Heaven, and the flag of heaven is the Cross."

During the ceremonies, Bishop Wood acted as celebrant and Bishop Neumann was his assistant. We can be sure that this secondary role disturbed Bishop Neumann not at all. He was happy that the building of the cathedral was progressing and the idea of having Bishop Wood as celebrant at the exercises may very well have been Bishop Neumann's own suggestion.

Things were progressing well in diocesan affairs, particularly in regard to financial problems, and this was due mainly to Bishop Wood's industry and zeal in coping with money matters. Bishop Wood apparently felt some unrest and impatience with his status as time went on, since he had the idea that Bishop Neumann would be leaving the diocese and he would be in charge. But the relationship between Bishop Wood and Bishop Neumann was cordial, even though, from Bishop Wood's point of view, he found it, at times, frustrating and irksome. To Bishop Wood's credit it must be said that he accepted the circumstances as they existed and prayerfully resigned himself to the will of God, as to his future status. And Bishop Wood's status, by the will of God, was soon to change.

On the morning of Thursday, January 5, 1860, Bishop Neumann was not feeling well. In fact, he had not been feeling well for the previous few days. But, no doubt mindful of his lifelong habit of never wasting a minute, he planned to take a walk and do a few errands. One of these errands was to check on a chalice which a priest in an outlying town had sent Bishop Neumann to be consecrated. Bishop Neumann had not received it, so he planned to inquire about it at the express office. He had assured the priest that, if the chalice was lost, he would see to it that the priest received another.

He had lunch with Bishop Wood and after lunch he received a visitor, one of his Redemptorist confreres, Father Urban. The visitor and Bishop Neumann chatted briefly. Noticing that Bishop Neumann did not look well, Father Urban inquired about his health.

"I have a strange feeling today," Bishop Neumann told him. "I feel as I never felt before. I have to go out on a little business and the fresh air will do me good."

Then he made a remark which puzzled Father Urban at the time.

"A man must always be ready," Bishop Neumann said, "for death comes when and where God wills it."

A short time later Bishop Neumann went on his errands. As he trod the Philadelphia streets he probably looked forward to continued improvement in all the situations which had been plaguing him since he became bishop eight years before. He probably planned, as soon as he felt better, to take up his duties with renewed vigor and zeal, increasing, as he went along, his harvest of souls.

But God had other plans for John Neumann. On that long-ago afternoon, the last soul to be delivered to his Creator by "The Little Bishop" was to be, very suddenly, his own.

CHAPTER SEVENTEEN

As he walked along Vine Street, near Thirteenth, his steps became uncertain and he was seen to stagger. A moment later he fell to the ground. Two strangers carried him into the home of a stranger, at 1218 Vine Street, and there, in a matter of minutes, he died.

Those who had tried to aid him noticed his episcopal cross and quickly sent word to Bishop Wood. A priest hurried to the scene to give "The Little Bishop" the last rites, but it was too late. Bishop Neumann, who had given the last rites to many departing souls, did not have this final consolation himself.

On examination of the body, it was discovered that Bishop Neumann wore, as a mortification, a metal belt, known as a cilicium. Father Tschenhens, his confessor, commenting on this, said: "Bishop Neumann was unrelenting in the practice of virtues of self-denial and mortification, but so prudently, so modestly did he act in this respect that such practices never attracted attention and never burdened anyone. He wore a girdle of iron wire that penetrated the flesh; he chastised his innocent body with a scourge which he had armed with a sharp nail; by interior recollection and constant guard over his eyes he shut out every temptation that could sully the purity of his heart so that his virginal soul uninterruptedly communed with God."

His wearing of the cilicium would never have been

known to the world if he had not died as he did, suddenly and, as far as his confreres were concerned, alone.

The news of Bishop Neumann's death spread quickly. Many did not believe it at first, since they knew of his vigor in making his visitation rounds and his description of himself as "a strong Bohemian mountain boy." But the newspapers confirmed the grim facts as news of "The Little Bishop's" passing was relayed to all parts of the country and abroad. Bishop Neumann had died of apoplexy in his forty-ninth year. In far-off Prachatitz Bishop Neumann's father heard of his son's passing, and no doubt it hastened his own death, several months later.

On the day after Bishop Neumann's death, Friday, January 6, the Feast of the Epiphany, the sad news was announced at all the Masses in the diocese. It was then that the full weight of the tragedy struck the hearts of the people. On Sunday, sermons on Bishop Neumann's life were preached from diocesan pulpits and his body, resting in the cathedral chapel, was viewed by thousands of mourners.

Great crowds of people watched the funeral procession on the following day. The cortege moved slowly from the episcopal chapel to St. John's Church. A delegation of police led the line of march, followed by a band with muffled instruments, hundreds of members of diocesan societies, and hundreds of priests and members of religious orders.

John Berger, the bishop's nephew, once wrote in a letter home: "He hated all honor and praise of the world." At his funeral, "The Little Bishop" had no choice. Honor and praise were showered upon him from all sides, from the rich and the poor, from the high and the low, from little children and from the aged. As the cortege moved through the streets, people at windows and on rooftops gazed down on the funeral hearse, drawn by four large black horses adorned with black plumes.

At St. John's, Bishop Wood sang the Requiem Mass and Archbishop Kenrick delivered the sermon. In a moving oration, Archbishop Kenrick told the congregation: "You will testify to his blameless life and unfeigned piety. The constant visitation of his diocese throughout almost the whole year marked him as the good shepherd anxious to afford his sheep the pastures of eternal life. . . . Truly he has been an active and devoted prelate, living only for his flock."

The people wept as Archbishop Kenrick paid tribute to his old friend. After the Requiem Mass, the cortege moved on to St. Peter's Church. Here, until late in the night, hundreds more of Bishop Neumann's people came to pay their respects. Bishop Wood celebrated another Requiem Mass the next morning at St. Peter's and then the body of "The Little Bishop" was entombed in the sanctuary vault of St. Peter's chapel.

This, in the usual course of events, would have been the end of Bishop Neumann's story. But, in his case, the course of events did not follow the usual pattern. Divergence from the usual pattern might have been noted at the funeral services. Many of those who came to mourn him sought to cut pieces from his robes, to preserve as relics. They were prevented from doing this, but later, out of their deep love for "The Little Bishop," the people began to make it a habit to pray at his tomb. Here, the thing that made this course of events unusual was the fact that they prayed, not *for* him, but *to* him. The people, especially the poor people who had been helped by his charity and his kindness, began to petition him for favors, for recovery from illness, for help with their many problems.

And, as the weeks and months went by, stories were heard and repeated, stories of the marvelous things which had come to pass after prayers had been addressed to Bishop Neumann, for his intercession before the throne of God.

The Church did not at this point sponsor the devotion to Bishop Neumann, nor did it take official action in the matter of recognizing any of the reported favors as coming as a result of prayer to "The Little Bishop." But, as time went on and the stories increased, the Church did focus attention on the matter.

In 1885, twenty-five years after the death of Bishop Neumann, application was made to Rome for the introduction of the cause of his beatification. A year later, what is known as "The Preparatory Process" was begun in Philadelphia and in Budweis. Ten years later, Pope Leo XIII accorded to Bishop Neumann the title of Venerable and, in 1921, Pope Benedict XV solemnly declared that Bishop Neumann had practiced the virtues in heroic degree and that further steps might be taken toward his beatification.

Pope Benedict, in making the Declaration of Heroicity, said: "We deem it proper to say that all our children should profit by the Decree of today by reason of the peculiar character of the heroic virtues of Ven. Neumann. Perhaps the very simplicity of these virtues has been misunderstood by those who thought there was no heroic degree in the virtues of the Servant of God, because in their eyes the good works and holy deeds performed by Neumann are the holy and good deeds which every good religious, every zealous missionary, every good bishop should perform.

"We need not repeat that works even the most simple, performed with constant perfection in the midst of inevitable difficulties, spell heroism in any servant of God. Just because of the simplicity of his works We find in them a strong argument for saying to the faithful of whatever age, sex or condition: You are all bound to imitate Ven. Neumann. . . .

"If in spite of this, there should be some who still seem surprised and cannot picture him to themselves as a hero apart from grand undertakings, We hasten to say that wonderful results can spring from simple deeds, provided these are performed as perfectly as possible and with unremitting constancy."

As the long, slow process towards Bishop Neumann's beatification continued, two miracles which resulted from prayer to "The Little Bishop" were approved by the Church.

On July 8, 1949, J. Kent Lenahan Jr., of Villanova, Pennsylvania, a music teacher and band leader, was critically injured in an automobile accident. His skull was crushed, one eye was almost torn from its socket, and he was bleeding from the ears, nose and mouth. At the hospital to which he was taken he lingered for four days between life and death. His condition was regarded as hopeless. He had a fever, with a 107-degree temperature and his pulse was 160.

His mother obtained a portion of the cassock of Bishop Neumann and applied it to her son. His temperature dropped to 100 degrees and his pulse rate was almost normal in a matter of hours. Within a few days his injuries were well on their way to complete healing and, five weeks after he entered the hospital, he was able to walk from the hospital unaided and to return home. He has enjoyed excellent health since that time.

In the town of Sassuolo, near Milan in northern Italy, an eleven-year-old girl named Eva Benassi was suffering from headaches, abdominal pains and fever. The time was May, 1923. Eva's doctor, Louis Barbante, diagnosed the case as tubercular peritonitis. Eva's condition grew steadily worse. One day Dr. Barbante told the little girl's relatives that death was imminent and could be expected that night. Eva and several nuns prayed for a cure to Venerable Bishop Neumann and that night all symptoms disappeared. When Dr. Barbante visited his patient the next morning he found Eva cured, without any sign of peritonitis. Eva, now more than fifty years old, enjoys good health.

These two cures played a major part in advancing the cause of Bishop Neumann toward beatification. He was beatified on October 13, 1963, when Pope Paul VI solemnly listed Bishop Neumann among the heavenly Blessed. His Redemptorist brethren, and all the people who had been praying for this honor for "The Little Bishop," not only in this country but in his native Prachatitz and other parts of the world, rejoiced in the good news.

Those who are familiar with the life story of Bishop Neumann might feel that he, so far as his own reactions were concerned, might be reluctant to have his name listed among the Blessed. But they would remember, too, that he was the type who would accept such honors, not for the glory of John Neumann, but for the glory of God.

In Philadelphia, even before the beatification of Bishop Neumann was announced, those who admired Bishop Neumann's life and who prayed to him for favors, inaugurated "The Neumann League of Prayer." His beatification now a fact, they pray for his canonization.

Bishop Neumann's canonization was brought closer to reality late in 1975, when news came from Rome that nine doctors, whose business it was to judge medical evidence for the Congregation for the Causes of Saints, declared that there was "no medical or scientific explanation" for the cure of Michael Flanigan, a 19-year-old New Jersey youth, who, some years previously, had cancer of the leg, jaw and lungs. The Flanigan family knew the explanation. They had prayed to Blessed John Neumann for the recovery of their son.

The tomb of Bishop Neumann in St. Peter's Church in Philadelphia is now the Blessed John Neumann Shrine. Philadelphians visit it and hundreds of people from other parts of the country and the world also come to pray at the shrine. Nearby is the Blessed John Neumann Museum, which contains his rosary, his chalice, his books and papers and other items. Surrounding the shrine are twenty-six stained-glass windows which illustrate highlights in Bishop Neumann's life.

At the shrine, and wherever admirers of Bishop Neumann kneel to meditate, they pray to "The Little Bishop," seeking favors through his heavenly intercession.

OLIVER PLUNKETT (In two parts)

I) *In His Own Words, by Desmond Forristal*
II) *Ireland's New Saint, by Tomas O'Fiaich*

Here is an absorbing look at another stormy period in Ireland, 300 years ago, in the story of its newest saint. Oliver Plunkett was one of the most controversial figures in a nation weaned on controversy. How his love for his people made him resolute in their defense, and the last man to be martyred for the Catholic faith in England, is an eloquent appeal for moderation today. Appendix gives places associated with the life of this saint, of special value to the pilgrim. Paper, no. 681, $3.95.

PADRE PIO

by Reverend John A. Schug, Capuchin

First really complete biography of the spiritual life of this modern "worker of miracles." Based on 7 years of research, including original notes and letters never before available. You'll be spellbound at this documented account of Padre Pio's miracles, his stigmata, his ability to be in two places at once, his gift of tongues, his constant visions, and his uncanny ability to read souls. Millions still flock to the little village in Italy where he lived and prayed, and where a religious hospital center is-growing fast. Paper, no. 856, $4.95.

ZEAL FOR YOUR HOUSE

by Bishop James E. Walsh
edited by Robert E. Sheridan, M.M.

What enables a man to endure 12 years of Chinese Communist imprisonment and then to emerge without bitterness or rancor? In this careful selection of previously unpublished writings and addresses, Bishop Walsh of Maryknoll gives a rare insight into the spirituality of a great modern missioner; tells what it is like to be a missioner and how converts are won. This book also offers a rare tribute to all great Catholic missioners — and to such places as Dunwoodie Seminary, Mount St. Mary's and St. Mary's Seminary. This is a rare treasury for everyone interested in the religious life and/or the Orient. Illustrated. Cloth, no. 792, $7.95.